Heroes of the Waves

The Boats & Coxswains
of
Fleetwood Lifeboat Station

Stephen Musgrave

David Pearce

Orchard Maritime Publications

Stalmine

First published 2017

Orchard Maritime Publications
Orchard Cottage,
Sarah's Fold,
Stalmine.
Poulton-le-Fylde
Lancashire

ISBN: 0993443237

ISBN-13: 978-0-9934432-3-7

DEDICATION

This book is dedicated to all those men and women, past and present who have helped to ensure that Fleetwood Lifeboat Station has been able to respond to all life-saving incidents at sea in the Morecambe Bay area during more than 160 years of service.

With courage, all things are possible:
William Hillary founder of the R.N.L.I.

Front Cover: Fleetwood Lifeboat *Kenneth James Pierpoint* was placed on station in June 2016. This depiction of Shannon Class lifeboat 13-14 passing Wyre Light in rough seas was painted by artist Ken Frost.

CONTENTS

ACKNOWLEDGMENTS

The authors would like to thank all those who helped in the production of this book.

Particular thanks to Artist Ken Frost for the paintings to illustrate this book and Ron Baxter for his pen and ink sketches.

Thanks to:

Ian Atkinson, John Dales, Margaret Minns and Rob Baines for use of their photographs.

Charles Wood and John Swannie for proof-reading the draft.
Dave Wright, Nicola Leadbetter and Carol Shuttleworth for responding with information on the Wright and Leadbetter families connected with the lifeboat station. Jeffrey Wright for information about his father.
John Bradbury M.B.E. for information on Morecambe Bay charts.

Derek Eaton and Lighthouse Stationers for digitizing the images.

Fleetwood Library, Lancashire Libraries & Information Services, Fleetwood Museum, Lancashire County Council Red Rose Collections, Evening Gazette, HMSO Admiralty Charts, for permission to use their resources.

Berkshire Family History Society for information on the Wasey family.

Fleetwood Lifeboat personnel of today and yesterday for their cooperation and time.

FOREWORD

Stephen and David have put a lot of work into this book, and must be commended for it.

We, the undersigned, have been involved with Fleetwood lifeboat Station for a combined total of more than 50 years and have seen some changes, new boats, new faces, new boathouse. We have also seen major change in the training and recruitment of volunteers and were closely involved in the introduction of some of them.

This book is a delightful collection of personal experiences, newspaper reports and the archives of the RNLI. It has been carefully collated to make an extremely interesting account of the history of Fleetwood Station since its inception all those years ago. It must have proved difficult to sort out fact from fiction, particularly in the early days when so few records were kept. The book takes us nicely up to the present day with the arrival of the latest class of lifeboat, coming to the Station in June 2016.

There are tales of daring-do from the records and also from the people involved and one can only wonder what it takes to produce people of this character and resourcefulness. We sometimes have to remind ourselves that these men and women are just volunteers.

How good it is to learn something of the people who man the lifeboats and, in particular, those who take command of these craft. We can only wonder at how they survived for hours spent at the oars striving to reach some stricken vessel, only to have to launch again to yet another in difficulties in the same storm. We learn of the little protection that they had in the early days and the hours spent soaked to the skin, cold, wet and hungry.

It is fascinating to read of the harbour tugs that were used to tow the early lifeboats out to sea in some terrible weather, after all they were designed for work close to the harbour and never designed to go to sea in such bad conditions.

We are confident that you will enjoy this book and the insight into the workings of such a worthy Institution. Anyone suggesting today that a service of such calibre could be set up and run using volunteers would think you crazy.

Captain David William Eccles, Master Mariner, MNI.

Captain Peter Woodworth, Extra Master, MSc., MNI.

PREFACE

The boats of the lifeboat service and the people who crew them are each heroic in their separate, yet complementary ways. For without their excellently designed and constructed boats the ordinary people who put to sea in them would be unable to perform their often gallant and extraordinary endeavours in saving lives at sea.

This book 'Heroes of the Waves' is focused on Fleetwood Lifeboat station but the human attributes of courage, vigilance, persistence, endurance, alertness and tenacity so essential in the lifeboat service are replicated in the 237 lifeboat stations around the coast of the United Kingdom and Ireland. For over 190 years people who have volunteered to crew the lifeboats have consistently sustained the values of never giving up even in extreme adversity, at times resulting in loss of life for the life-savers themselves.

Over the past two centuries the lifeboats have been transformed from rowing and sailing vessels with little protection from the elements for the crew, to high speed craft packed with technology where the crew are sheltered in an air conditioned cabin on hydraulic suspension seats with harness straps to enable them to get to the location of a casualty up to 100 miles from the shore and with pin-point navigational accuracy. In the nineteenth and twentieth century the crew were often volunteers from the local seafaring community who possessed knowledge and skills of seamanship. From the latter part of the twentieth century the men and women who volunteer to crew the lifeboats may not have such knowledge initally but the lifeboat service now operates its own college to train individuals and develop the necessary skills and competence to crew the lifeboats.

Dramatic rescues justly receive acclaim both locally and nationally but in the 24 x 7 operation every day of the year around the entire coastline the less publicised activities of the service include many long tows home in dreary weather, all-night searches and assistance for broken down vessels. In each of these cases however mundane the task may appear the lifeboat crews' response is rapid and attentive because for each of these people in difficulties the appearance of the lifeboat to assist them is nothing less than a life-saving event.

The book considers each of the lifeboats at Fleetwood station over the past almost 160 years. A small number of notable actual rescue incidents are given for each lifeboat, accompanied by a vignette portrayal of each of the lifeboat coxswains over this period. In the early chapters the descriptions of events are drawn from press reportage of the time and fortunately the newspaper articles were exceptionally detailed, although some of the language appears somewhat quaint but is largely unaltered to convey the sense of that period in time.

From the stories of actual rescue incidents over the past century and a half it can be seen that the boats have changed beyond recognition but the people who are prepared to crew them remain the same, as the lifeboats are still crewed by volunteers.

This book is not intended as a history of the Lifeboat Service in Fleetwood; each chapter considers a different period in time and features a small number of the more outstanding rescues undertaken by individual lifeboats on station, along with a pen portrait of each of the coxswains of the Fleetwood Lifeboats, give a human insight into the people of the Fleetwood Lifeboat station and their crew. The story of the Fleetwood Lifeboat station is one of dedication and commitment to the cause of lifesaving. For over 160 years, lifeboat crews have carried out rescues around Morecambe Bay, with a number of instances that led to recognition and award of medals and vellum certificates for outstanding bravery.

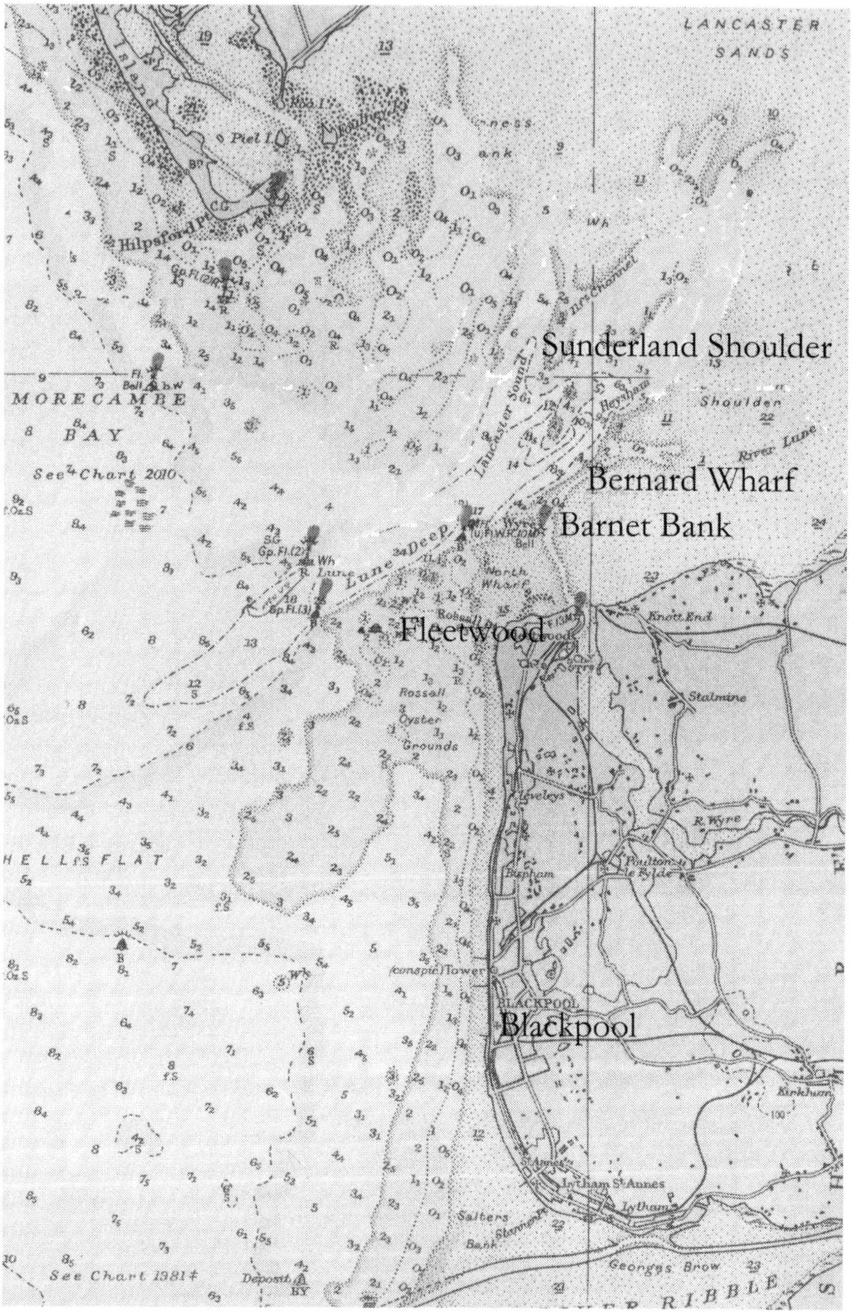

Chart of Morecambe Bay Courtesy Admiralty Charts

1 THE FIRST LIFEBOAT AT FLEETWOOD (1859 – 1862)

When the weather is fine and visibility is clear the rugged prospect of the Lakeland hills forms a dramatic backdrop behind the northern shore of Morecambe Bay (on the Lancashire coast of Northwest England). By contrast the southern shores of the same bay are flatlands, with low profile and sandbanks that extend for miles at low tide. In this bay the sandy floor of Lune Deeps (a former glacial river-bed) continues to offer a safe anchorage on the sloping sides for vessels to shelter from southwesterly gales during stormy weather. Few rocks exist around this coast yet the sandy seabed remains an unforgiving shoreline, where many vessels have perished as tremendous seas pounded them on this hard ground.

Since pre-Roman times vessels have plied the shores of Morecambe Bay, trading into the small ports and creeks, transporting cargo and people along the coast. Records show that mishaps have frequently happened but before the inception of the lifeboat service any hope of rescue was down to what local vessels and crew might be nearby to assist but there was no coordinated sea rescue system.

For those people who volunteer to crew the lifeboats pride in the lifeboat service derives through a complex combination of feelings. Participation in sea rescues that in themselves sometimes involve life and death incidents; the opportunity to be part of a close team that is committed to a worthwhile pursuit of saving human life and the satisfaction of serving on the finest craft that can be built for withstanding extremes of weather in hazardous sea conditions are motivating factors. The physical lifeboats and crew members uniquely complement each other; the feeling of confidence in the lifeboats themselves as a safe platform and deck upon which to venture upon the stormy sea enables normal men and women to perform outstanding acts of bravery in saving lives that might otherwise be lost if the boats and crews were not available.

Everything about Fleetwood was brand new back in Victorian times. It was a town created from a greenfield site by the local Squire, Sir Peter Hesketh Fleetwood and designed by Decimus Burton, a noted architect of the day and a friend of Sir Peter's.

Building work began in 1835 on a desolate site which had been a giant rabbit warren on the Lancashire coast where the river Wyre flows into Morecambe Bay – part of the Irish Sea. But this remote peninsula location was already well known to mariners. The phrase: " as safe as Wyre water" had been coined to underline the natural anchorage available in the Wyre to ships sheltering from the fierce westerly winds that could drive a hapless vessel into the shallow waters of Morecambe Bay and force it aground where stormy seas could then pound it to matchwood and condemn the crew to a watery grave.

There is evidence that the Romans and the Vikings were active in this part of Lancashire known as the Fylde which takes in the coast south of Fleetwood where the towns of Cleveleys and Blackpool lie and extends to St Annes and Lytham at the mouth of the River Ribble. Southport and the Mersey estuary lie further south.

Sir Peter wanted to develop an industrial town linked by the Preston and Wyre Railway to the mainline at Preston. He envisaged enclosed docks but he also wanted Fleetwood to be a resort – not just for the gentry but for the working folk of industrial Lancashire who had helped to build the industrial revolution. It is thought that Fleetwood was the first town in the world to welcome seaside visitors by train. They came on a Sunday which was their only free day from work in the textile factories in the smoky cotton towns.

The Preston and Wyre line opened in 1840 but when Blackpool joined the system six years later, businessmen there began to offer more attractions than the sea, the beach and the fresh air and so the world-famous resort was born. Financially, Fleetwood cost Sir Peter dear and, although not all the grand design came to fruition, the town he dreamed of was born and survived.

Another new feature of life in England in those days was Her Majesty's Coastguard service. In 1809 the Preventative Water Guard had been formed by the government. Their job was to combat smuggling – especially in the south with its close links to France. But there was also a duty to help the victims of shipwreck. By 1822 the title Coast Guard appeared in official documents under the control of the Board of Customs. By the 1850's, with smuggling on the wane, the Coastguard came under the control of the Admiralty with a one-word title. Their mission now was to save lives, take charge of wrecks and protect property.

The new town of Fleetwood was quickly chosen as one base for this new-look maritime force and a detachment of Coastguards were based there. Today, the terrace of sturdy, brick-built cottages where they were quartered are sought after as attractive modern homes or let to holidaymakers as a summer base. At one end of the terrace, in Abbotts Walk, is a much more substantial house which has been the home of a retired local doctor for many years.

This was once the home of Captain Edward Wasey R.N., the Inspecting Officer of the Fleetwood Coastguard and a man who was to play a pivotal role in Fleetwood's proud heritage of saving life at sea. The Coastguard houses lay in the shadow of The Mount which was the largest of the sand-hills along the shore and was later developed into a public park. The modern promenade with its fine views of the Lake District mountains and the seafront gardens and attractions of a typical small seaside resort were things of the future. The sea lay close by and it's thought that a creek led inland so that small craft could be berthed at the rear of the cottages.

There was also a training facility for Royal Navy Reservists using gunnery targets nearby on the shore. It may have been the case that Captain Wasey was on half pay because no sea going role was available for him. He was well aware of the work of the Royal National Lifeboat Institution which had been founded in 1824 by Sir William Hillary although independent lifesaving teams had been operating in various locations long before.

In the early years, the number of lifeboat stations grew only slowly and were often established because of appeals to the R.N.L.I. by local residents. In 1858 Captain Wasey wrote to the Lifeboat Institution's

London headquarters pleading Fleetwood's cause. In November that year the Lifeboat Institution's management committee agreed to establish a station at Fleetwood. Captain Wasey was the first Honorary Secretary and one of his Coastguards, John Fox, was the first Coxswain.

A new lifeboat was allocated to Fleetwood and delivered to the town on a railway wagon, arriving on 8th February, 1859. Their boat was built by Forestt of Limehouse in London and cost £140 and one shilling. She was 30 feet long and 6 foot 3 inches beam; a six oared 'Peake' class self-righting lifeboat built by T&W Forrestt of Limehouse, London. Since the late medieval times Limehouse, on the River Thames, had become a significant port with extensive docks and wharves, with related industries such as shipbuilding. However, as the age of steam of the nineteenth century led to the building of bigger ships, the facilities at Limehouse became inadequate. Local ingenuity then found a highly successful alternative in building smaller boats and many of the Royal National Lifeboat Institution's lifeboats were built in Limehouse between 1852 and 1890. The Fleetwood lifeboat was built to a design by James Beeching, a boat-builder from Bexhill who trained in Hastings and had been involved in the smuggling world when he was younger. In 1851 he won an international competition for the design of a self-righting lifeboat which was modified slightly by James Peake, a master shipwright at the Woolwich dockyard. So the first Fleetwood boat was a Beeching-Peake Self-Righter.

A further £174 18 shillings and six pence was spent on a boathouse on the shore opposite the North Euston Hotel which was built by local businessman Frederick Kemp – a man who was active in the development of the town in Fleetwood's early days. He had been agent to Sir Peter Hesketh Fleetwood who spent a great deal of his considerable fortune on his new town of Fleetwood before leaving to spend his latter years in London.

Fleetwood's first lifeboat does not appear to have been given a name and only went out on nine service launches during her three years at the port. But she and her crew saved 32 lives and placed Fleetwood firmly on the map at R.N.L.I. headquarters. Captain Wasey played a leading role in all this ashore and afloat and was awarded no less than three silver medals by the Institution for his courage and skill.

Captain Wasey's family home was far from the sea – by the Thames in Newbury, Berkshire. The well-to do family had a tradition of philanthropy. Back in 1862 Miss Mary Wasey of Newbury gave the RNLI £340 for a bigger and better Fleetwood boat with a new launching carriage. At her request, it was named *Edward Wasey* as a tribute to the leadership and courage of the man who established Fleetwood's proud reputation as a lifeboat station.

Once again, the boat was built at the Forestt yard and was bigger than its predecessor. This time there were 10 oars to power a 32-foot craft with a beam of 7 feet 11 inches. The bill was £224 16 shillings and 6 pence with an additional £90 8 shillings for the launching carriage.

The London and North Western Railway Company provided free transport for the craft and equipment from London to Fleetwood.

The Wasey Family

Miss Mary Wasey must have been one of the most generous donors the Royal National Lifeboat Institution has ever known.

After her death in 1880 a local newspaper reported that she had presented: " no less than six or seven lifeboats with their transporting carriages" to the R.N.LI.

And it seems likely that her great support for the Institution and its crews began when a relative, Edward Wasey, a Captain the Royal Navy, played a vital part in the birth and early work of Fleetwood's R.N.L.I. station.

But the story seems to start with Mary's brother, John Thomas Wasey, a lawyer from Newbury in Berkshire whose fortune enabled him to buy an old country house and estate called Priors Court in the ancient country parish of Chieveley near Newbury. The story of the land and houses on the site could be traced back to medieval times.

At the 1851 census John was described as a Deputy Lieutenant of the County, a Magistrate, the owner of 600 acres and the employer of 25 men and five women. He died, unmarried, in 1852 without making a will and his estate passed to Mary and her widowed sister, Mrs Jane Stacpoole, who both lived near Newbury. The two women did a great deal for charity from building a village school to supporting the work of various hospitals.

In the 1871 census, Mary is described as a gentlewoman and landowner and head of the household at Priors Court which she shared with five domestic servants. When Mary died in 1880, Captain Wasey – or Edward Frodsham Noel Kindersley Wasey to give him his full title – inherited part of her considerable estate.

In retirement, he lived near Maidenhead and, when he died in 1902 at the age of 82, was buried in the churchyard of St Michael's church in the Thames-side village of Bray – now home to stars of the entertainment world and a very famous restaurant.

As for Priors Court it became a private school and is now a residential centre and school for young people with autism – work that Mary and Jane would probably have approved of.

They are remembered through stained glass windows in the chapel at Curridge which is part of Chieveley parish and they depict six acts of mercy mentioned in the bible – help for the hungry, thirsty, naked, sick, homeless and imprisoned.

Dreadful Gales in Morecambe Bay January 22nd 1860

In the first month of 1860 the newspaper headlines and reportage from that time show that Morecambe Bay was affected by stormy weather with gale force winds frequently blowing. Shipping had been disrupted and sailings cancelled due to the stormy weather around the UK coast. Strong South Westerly winds and heavy rain had swept across the Fylde coast throughout Thursday 19th January, 1860. As dawn broke on the next day (Friday morning) towering anvil clouds were rapidly approaching from the West, causing gusting winds from the North West, accompanied by showers of hailstones. The gale continued to rage on the coast on Saturday night 21st January and throughout Sunday 22nd January. It was the most severe gale that had been known in

Fleetwood for many years. Few people could remember anything like it and the disasters around the North West coast caused by the gale were dreadful. On Saturday afternoon the wind rose to full gale force from the West South West, and threatened danger to unsheltered vessels. A barque, the *Tyne*, of Newcastle, bound for Glasson Dock laden with grain for Mr Rawsthorne, a corn merchant of Preston, had been lying at anchor off Fleetwood for five or six days waiting for the Spring Tides *(Spring Tides cause higher water levels at full moon and new moon, followed by Neap Tides of more moderated levels around seven days later than Spring Tides)* to enable her to enter the dock at Glasson. The adverse weather prevented this and around 4.00 p.m. on Sunday afternoon and with Pilot John Grimshaw on board she slipped her anchor to seek shelter at Fleetwood instead. Under the skilful management of Pilot Grimshaw she was brought into Fleetwood in the protected waters of the harbour. The skill and judgement shown by the pilot in bringing the barque *Tyne* safely into port was praised by the authorities, as the harbour was so crowded with shipping on that day. Many other vessels had also been brought into the sheltered waters until the storm abated and to steer the barque in the gale that was blowing, without sustaining or causing any damage, was a feat worthy of commendation. As the day advanced the gale increased and before midnight a violent storm force 11 wind was blowing. The lightering flat barge *Arthur*, laden with coal, belonging to Mr W. Atkinson, sank in the river in front of the Lower Lighthouse on the Esplanade but neither of her crew were in her at the time.

For three days the anchorage inside the harbour was full with vessels that had delayed their departure due to the severe weather and others that had sought shelter from the storm in the relatively new port of Fleetwood.

On Sunday morning, a barque was riding with two anchors down near the King Scar buoy, and was low in the water with several feet of water in her hold. She was the *Charles Brunell*, on passage from Singapore to Liverpool, with the general cargo of East Indian merchandise. The steam tug *Adjutant* took her in tow but being heavily laden, with nine feet of water in her bilges, the power of the *Adjutant* was insufficient to be of much service to her. The *Adjutant* continued to have difficulty controlling her tow in the strong current with the *Charles Brunell* broadside to the weather in the Wyre channel. The windage caused the barque to run aground, striking the eastern side of the channel on Bernard Wharf. Her crew decided to remain on board, confident that they could refloat her on the next tide.

The *Adjutant*, unable to assist further then left the disabled barque and proceeded to meet the barque *Tallula,* laden with cotton from Savannah. She had entered the bay a short time earlier and was heading for the Wyre Lighthouse, making signals for a pilot. Mr McLean, the pilot, was put on board the *Tallulah* and she was brought to anchor just to the Westward of the Wyre light.

Later on Sunday morning another large three-masted vessel came into sight, tacking to get around the North Wharf, soon anchoring in a place of comparative safety between Wyre Lighthouse and King Scar. She was the *Victoria*, outward bound from Liverpool to Mobile, U.S.A. but now seeking shelter in Morecambe Bay. Towards evening the wind again rose and threatened fresh dangers to the vessels at anchor in the bay. A little before 6.00 p.m. on that Sunday evening, blue lights were seen burning and rockets ascending into the night sky as signals of distress from a vessel between Shell Wharf and the Kings Scar bank. These were answered from the Coast Guard station by response signals and Mr Fox, the lifeboat coxswain, gave the order to 'take out the lifeboat'. A volunteer crew was very soon found and notwithstanding the danger and the darkness the boat was launched a short time after the distress signals were seen. Captain Wasey, of the Coastguard service, accompanied the crew. The crew rowed down the channel but in the darkness and with stormy conditions they were making little progress as the floodtide was then running strongly against them. They lit a flare to signal for the assistance of the steam-tug *Adjutant* to take the lifeboat in tow. As soon as steam pressure was raised Captain William Swarbrick, Master of the steam tug, promptly followed the lifeboat and took her in tow. As the tug and lifeboat were passing the *Charles Brunell*, still aground at the edge of the Wyre channel, Mr. Hornby, the pilot on-board *Charles Brunell*, hailed the lifeboat coxswain, informing him that they had just seen a schooner run aground on the north point of Bernard Wharf; but he knew nothing further of her.

Thinking that the crew of the schooner on Bernard Wharf had a better chance of surviving than those on board the vessel towards Shell Wharf that had sent up distress rockets, the decision was taken on the lifeboat to continue towards the original ship that had indicated its distress at Shell Wharf. Once clear of the Fleetwood channel the tug *Adjutant* released the lifeboat, which raised its sails and headed Westward towards King Scar. With the pilot, Mr. Gerard, on board the *Adjutant*, the tug then steamed to the *Victoria* that was at anchor off King Scar. After some initial difficulty the pilot was put on board her by transferring him using a hauling line. It was truly an awful night, the like of which had never been experienced in the Bay before. The *Adjutant* could now scarcely make any headway against the wind and tide but continued towards the lifeboat to see if further assistance was required. Heavy seas were breaking right over the lifeboat, which was being tossed about violently and despite repeated tacking was finding it impossible to overcome the wind and adverse tide. Making little Westerly progress the coxswain and crew on-board the lifeboat began to realise that it was becoming impossible to reach Shell Wharf due to the extreme weather. The coxswain consulted with Captain Wasey and having reached a decision the lifeboat coxswain gave the order to turn around, to return to the schooner that had earlier foundered on Bernard Wharf.

The lifeboat reached the location of the schooner shortly before 9.00 p.m.. She was found to be the *Ann Mitchell*, of Montrose, on passage from Sligo, with a cargo of oats for Liverpool. She had sailed from Sligo, on the West coast of Ireland, on the 10th January with Captain James Chalmers as Skipper, John Barclay as Mate, along with a crewman John Miggleston, and a ship's boy Alexander Macpherson.

The schooner had encountered severe weather on her passage, and about 5:30 p.m. on Sunday evening, being unfamiliar with the coastline and not knowing their position, their vessel ran aground on the North-West point of Bernard Wharf. As cresting seas broke over her all her deck lumber, binnacle, compass, windlass, and almost everything on the upper deck was swept away by the sea washing completely over her as the floodtide was then making. The sea washing aft across the deck ripped the binnacle from its mountings and it toppled over striking crewman Miggleston, who was at the helm steering their vessel, breaking both his legs. The skipper signaled their distress hoisting an ensign upside down from the mast, but no relief came until much later on. The schooner's boat was not seaworthy in such gale force conditions, so the crew took to the rigging, waiting for assistance.

Lifeboat launching to assist crew of Schooner *Ann Mitchell*

As the lifeboat approached the wrecked schooner a heavy sea broke over the lifeboat and nearly filled the boat, at the same time breaking two of her oars. The lifeboat quickly dropped its anchor and an attempt was made to get the crew off from the windward side. Lines were thrown to them but with the tide sweeping past along the bank at the rate of five or six knots it wasn't possible to get anyone off from this side. Efforts were then made to approach and get close to the vessel on its leeward side, but as the lifeboat was being manoeuvred around the hull the schooner rolled over on her beam ends, her masts nearly falling on the lifeboat. After narrowly escaping the masts and rigging the coxswain stood off to re-assess the situation. He quickly decided to re-anchor the lifeboat to windward and veer down until nearly touching the wreck. Lines and a lifebuoy were then thrown to the crew, and one line fastened to the vessel. The crew of the lifeboat hearing the word given to haul, pulled away on the line but they found it had been tied on to the vessel by one of the ship's crew. The lifebuoy line was next hauled in, and one man, the Mate, was thus saved. He was quite insensible and only semi-conscious when he was rescued and had to be resuscitated. The others in the vessel appeared unable to assist themselves with the lifeline, or feared to throw themselves over the schooners side. The cries of the unfortunate men on board the schooner were heart rending to those on the lifeboat, and it could be seen that a scuffle was taking place among them for possession of the lifeline. Those remaining on the schooner continued their attempts to save themselves using the life-line but wave after wave hampered their efforts and they all lost their lives. Mate Barclay told his rescuers that crewman Miggleston had two broken legs and other injuries. Skipper Chalmers had earlier injured his back and the boy, Alexander MacPherson, had died. Heavy seas at that moment broke over both the wreck and the lifeboat, with the breaking wave carrying the lifeboat and its anchor uncontrollably away from the schooner until she was some 300 yards away from the ship. Only with great difficulty were the lifeboat crew able to retrieve the anchor and row back to the schooner's devastated hull. Not a living soul could be seen as they approached the capsized hull that had been turned upside down. The vessel had originally fallen over on her beam ends but was now turned keel upwards and nothing more was seen of the skipper or anyone else on board.

All this time the tug *Adjutant* with Captain Swarbrick and his crew had been searching in the Bay for the lifeboat. The navigation lights of the lifeboat had been blown out, and could not be re-lit in the extreme conditions. Two hours later and soon after midnight the steam tug located the lifeboat in the vicinity of the wrecked schooner and with difficulty got alongside to pass a towrope and took her in tow towards the harbour. All the lifeboat crew agreed that they never experienced such a night in their lifetime, their limbs being quite numbed by the cold conditions. As they returned up the Wyre channel the steam tug and the lifeboat crew also made an attempt to get the *Charles Brunell* off the sandbank, but could not move her an inch, as she had now well over 9 feet of water in her bilges. A sail was therefore hoisted on-board the *Charles Brunell* to keep her on the bank and prevent the barque from floating into deep water, where she would inevitably have sunk.

The schooner wreck of the *Ann Mitchell* lay in a position on the sandbanks of Bernard Wharf, where it was dry over the banks at low-water. On Monday evening James Turner, one of the lifeboat crew, and John Barclay the Mate who had been rescued from the *Ann Mitchell* walked out across the sands to the wreck to see if any bodies could be found. They found the schooner's hull had broken in two, and it's keel turned upwards. Forcing an entrance through the battered timbers of the hull they discovered one body. It was that of the Skipper James Chalmers, shockingly mutilated, with a lifeline made fast round his waist. The unfortunate skipper's clothing had been pulled up above his head and his trousers and undergarments pulled below his feet by the rope action inside the upturned hull. The body was taken to the Bourne Arms hotel, at Knott End to await an inquest. The skipper, James Chalmers, whose body had been recovered, had left a wife but no children.

Early on Monday morning many people had gone up onto the promenade hoping to learn something of the nights disasters, and to know how the vessel seen on the previous day had stood up to the gale. The *Victoria* had weathered the storm, riding safely at anchor on the side of Lune Deeps, off King Scar. This was not the case for the *Jane Roper*; the schooner that signaled her distress on the previous evening by a blue distress lights and rockets on the Shell Wharf. She belonged to Ulverston, Cumbria, and was bound from Newport for Morecambe, under the command of William Harris, with a crew of four men and a boy. The lifeboat was again launched and the tug *Adjutant*, with Captain William Swarbrick, took her in tow. At 10 o'clock that morning the lifeboat was cast off from the steam tug. After two unsuccessful attempts to take off the men from the *Jane Roper*, aground on Shell Wharf, the lifeboat was being pushed further to leeward by the strong current. The lifeboat had to be taken in tow again and pulled to windward by the steam tug, to enable her to veer down onto the vessel again. Fortunately, the lifeboat eventually took off the whole crew who were in a very exhausted state. They had not eaten any food or had anything to drink for three days. Although they had been sheltering beneath the lowered sails strewn on deck, the sails had offered little protection from the gale. They were landed at noon in Fleetwood, where an immense crowd had gathered on the beach to witness their arrival. The volunteer crew of the lifeboat were praised for their gallant exertions, along with the Captain and crew of the steam-tug *Adjutant*, for their gallant conduct during Sunday and Monday.

The inquest on the body of James Chalmers, Master of the *Ann Mitchell* was held at the Bourne Arms Hotel, Knott End on Wednesday 31st January, before a Coroner. John Barclay, of Montrose, the mate, had previously identified the body of the deceased. James Turner, having been sworn in, said that he was on the crew of the lifeboat on Sunday 22nd January. A signal of distress being observed on the vessel between Shell Wharf and the King Scar bank, the lifeboat put off to give assistance. On passing a barque in the river a pilot on board told them that the schooner was aground on Bernard Wharf point. The lifeboat crew, thinking the vessel at Shell Wharf was in a more dangerous position than the deceased's schooner, made way down past King Scar. They could not get far due to a strong adverse current, and therefore turned about and went Eastwards to the *Anne Mitchell.* The crew had climbed up the rigging when the lifeboat reached them, and a lifeline and lifebelts were thrown to them. After much difficulty, one man, the previous witness, was hauled into the lifeboat. The second line having been made fast to something, restraining the lifeboat, the lifeboat crew had to let go the end of it. Suddenly, the vessel capsized and nothing more was seen of those on board. The witness James Turner and another man walked out to the wreck on Monday night, and succeeded in recovering the body of the deceased, which was entangled in a rope under the rigging. The coroner then briefly addressed the jury on the case, and the verdict of accidentally drowned was returned.

For this rescue from the schooner *Ann Mitchell*, Captain Wasey R.N., who was the Honorary Secretary of the lifeboat and lifeboat coxswain John Fox, who was chief boatman for the Coastguard station at Fleetwood, were awarded the Silver Medal of the National Lifeboat Institution.

Later in the week more than a dozen men were taken out and put on board the *Charles Brunell* to assist in sorting out this barque. Small lightering barges were towed out to enable her cargo to be discharged in preparation for re-floating her. The crew were signed off and left her at Fleetwood and a replacement crew were sent. When re-floated on the next Spring tides she was towed by tug to Liverpool.

Schooner *Catherine* stranded on Bernard Wharf 19th February, 1860

Within a month of the previous incident, on Saturday evening 18th February, 1860, the schooner *Catherine*, of Newry, under the command of Captain McDonald, with a cargo of wooden pit props, anchored near Wyre Lighthouse for the night. The Master had earlier refused the assistance of the steam tug to tow his vessel into Fleetwood. By Sunday morning the weather had changed, with the wind rising to gale force, causing the anchor cable to part. The schooner was driven by the West North West wind right on to Bernard Wharf. The tide was about three quarters flood at the time.

As dawn broke soon after 8 o'clock in the morning, from the shore at Fleetwood a signal of distress was observed from her. Mr Fox, the lifeboat coxswain, ordered the lifeboat to be manned to render assistance. At the time of launching a heavy sea was running at the launching site. Before the lifeboat was clear of the launching carriage a breaking wave struck the lifeboat, instantly filling it with sea water and throwing it broadside on to the beach. The lifeboat was quickly recovered and hauled back onto the transporting carriage. On the second attempt the lifeboat and crew, accompanied by Capt Wasey, was launched; the crew with oars in hand. The crew had been thoroughly soaked when the boat filled with water. Without time to change or dry themselves off they rowed down the Wyre channel. After about an hour of hard pulling at the oars in the teeth of the heavy gale, with the tide running between five and six knots, the disabled schooner *Catherine* was reached. Three of the men were quickly taken off from the weather quarter. The skipper was next hauled to the lifeboat by means of a lifeline. One of the schooner's men had his head injured when he was in the lifeboat. In his exhausted condition he had rested his head on the gunwhale. As the lifeboat was rising on a wave his head struck the schooners boom, severely injuring his skull and one of his ears. About 11:30 a.m. the lifeboat with the crew from the wrecked vessel arrived in Fleetwood and the injured man's wounds were promptly attended to. Before the lifeboat went out, a sailing boat from the harbour set out to the stranded schooner, but, because the lifeboat had reached them, put back without having taken any one off the wreck. The behaviour of the lifeboat was very highly spoken of on the occasion. Within the period of one month, this same lifeboat, manned by Capt Wasey, R.N., and her coxswain, John Fox, had been instrumental in saving 10 persons from the wrecked vessels, *Jane Roper*, *Ann Mitchell*, and the *Catherine*. For this rescue Captain Wasey was awarded a Silver clasp to his previous Silver medal.

Vessel *Vermont* Saturday October 20th 1860

On Saturday morning 20th October, 1860, the ship *Vermont* of Halifax and laden with timber was laying at anchor near the Wyre Light. The wind at the time was blowing fresh to strong with a full tide flowing. The combination of wind and tide was too much for her, putting excessive strain on the chains even with both anchors out. First one, then soon afterwards the second of her anchor chains parted and she drifted south-eastwards and grounded high up on Bernard Wharf, not that far from the Little Ford, where the East India man, *Charles Brunell*, was stranded in January of the same year. As the tide rose the ship drifted higher on the bank and every sea washed completely over her hull. The Fleetwood lifeboat was then launched to take the crew off, consisting of the Captain and 14 men, and the Pilot on board, Mr McLean. The steam tug *Adjutant*, with Captain Swarbrick, took the lifeboat in tow. Shortly afterwards all aboard the *Vermont* were taken safely off the disabled ship onto the lifeboat. The captain, who was part owner, secured his papers before leaving his vessel. As the storm passed and the wind reduced the lifeboat was again manned to take the Captain back on board his ship to get possession of her. However, part of the crew of a diver's smack had boarded her, and put in a claim against the ship. The captain of the *Vermont* was put on board to resolve this dispute. Later that week a portion of the ship's cargo transferred to flat lightering barges and brought to Fleetwood, where the vessel herself was brought on the next spring tides. The conduct of the divers who had boarded the *Vermont* was the main topic of discussion in the town during that week, causing the divers to abandon any claim on the vessel.

In little over 18 months since the lifeboat station had been established the un-named lifeboat had been involved in rescuing 27 persons in very stormy weather from the wrecked vessels - *Ann Mitchell* of Montrose, the *Catherine*, of Newry, the *Jane Roper*, of Ulverston; and the barque *Vermont*, of Halifax.

Captain Wasey was Inspecting Commander of Coast Guard; and Coxswain Fox, had on each occasion been out in the lifeboat. For his part in this rescue Captain Wasey was awarded by the National Lifeboat Institution a second Silver clasp to his Silver Medal.

Coxswain John Fox and Capt Edward Wasey. 1859-1862.

Beyond the narrative in the above pages there is little reportage of coxswain John Fox and Captain Edward Wasey in the local newspaper of the time.

The Loss of the Fleetwood Lifeboat 23rd October, 1862.

On the morning of Thursday 23rd October 1862 the Fleetwood lifeboat was called out in severe weather to assist a schooner that was seen to be in difficulties in the storm, South West of Blackpool. Some portions of the vessel's sail were still set, giving rise to a belief that her crew were still alive on board. The vessel gradually drifted nearer the coast until around 2 miles from the shore where she struck the ground and soon sank, with only her masts visible above the waves.

The Fleetwood Lifeboat was taken in tow by the steam-tug *Wyre*, commanded by Captain William Swarbrick. Off Blackpool the winds were of severe gale force and the sea was reported as running 'mountains high and curling over in a frightful manner', and it was decided to take the crew of the lifeboat on board the tug. Having transferred the lifeboat crew safely on board the tug *Wyre* in the worsening sea conditions the lifeboat capsized twice but being self-righting she rolled back upright again. When the steam-tug *Wyre*, still towing the lifeboat, arrived at the wreck they found the vessel had sunk, with just the masts visible.

Loss of the Fleetwood Lifeboat

Nothing could be seen or heard of the stranded vessels crew, so after searching the area the tug and lifeboat believing they could be of no further assistance turned back towards Fleetwood.

The wind had risen to storm force on the slow return journey, when in Lune Deeps and darkness the tow-rope parted, leaving the empty lifeboat drifting off into the blackness. The weather was so bad that the crew of the steam-tug *Wyre* quickly abandoned the search and with the lifeboat crew still on board headed back for Fleetwood, having sustained some damage to her superstructure and deck-houses.

Later that week the Fleetwood lifeboat was washed ashore in the north of Morecambe Bay, and arrangements were made to return the damaged hull to Fleetwood by train on a railway truck. Serious damage had been done to her port side, which had been broken open, besides other damage done to her interior.

This first lifeboat had only been on station at Fleetwood for three years since February 1859. At a meeting of the Lifeboat Committee, it was resolved to make application to the National Lifeboat Institution for a ten-oar'd boat, that would be better suited to the local conditions than the previous one.

Although he was not a member of the R.N.L.I lifeboat crew William Swarbrick played an essential role as Captain of the harbour tug *'Wyre'* that routinely took the 'rowing and sailing' lifeboat in tow, often in extreme weather conditions. Captain William Swarbrick and the crew of the tug *'Wyre'* were back in action the following week on 27th October, 1862, when in the absence of the lost Fleetwood lifeboat they rescued the Captain and thirteen crew of the barque *Pudyona*, of Glasson Dock, Lancaster.

Captain Swarbrick and Pilot Robert Gerrard both received Silver medals from the lifeboat service for this rescue. Captain Swarbrick also received an inscribed telescope from the government.

Record of Service Rendered by the un-named first Fleetwood Lifeboat lifeboat (1859-1862)

August 30th, 1859. First call out *Sir Colin Campbell* WNW gale. Ship reached port unaided.

January 22nd, 1860. Schooner *Ann Mitchell* of Montrose ran aground and total wreck – rescued sole survivor. Coxswain John Fox and Captain Edward Wasey Silver Medal.

January 23rd 1860. Schooner *Jane Roper* saved 5.

February 19th, 1860. Schooner *Catherine* of Newry. Full gale, heavy snow, violent seas. Saved 6. Captain Edward Wasey Second Silver Medal.

October 20th, 1860. Barque *Vermont* of Nova Scotia, wrecked on Bernard Wharf. Violent WNW gale. Saved 15 plus Pilot. Captain Wasey 3rd Silver Medal.

November 2nd, 1860 Sloop *Britannia* of Barrow. Aground on North Wharf. Ultimately lifeboat not needed.

November 11th, 1860. Brig *Sister Anne* of Whitehaven. Reported in difficulties on Bernard Wharf. Ultimately lifeboat not required.

October 23rd, 1862. Loss of first Fleetwood Lifeboat.

October 27th, 1862. Barque *Pudyona* of Glasson. No lifeboat on station. Captain William Swarbrick in Tug *Wyre* rescued crew.

This page is intentionally blank

2 THE EARLY PULLING & SAILING LIFEBOATS (1862 – 1894)

Lifeboat *'Edward Wasey'* (1862-1879)

The replacement for the lifeboat lost on 23rd October, 1862, arrived on station at Fleetwood three weeks later in November 1862. A gift of £340 from Miss Mary Wasey of Newbury paid for the construction of the 10 oared self-righting lifeboat. The lifeboat was named *Edward Wasey* and was 32 foot long and 7 foot 11 inches beam. Built by Forrest in London at a cost of £226 16s 6d for the boat and £90 8s 0d for the carriage.

James Leadbetter coxswain 1862 – 1869

James was a fisherman who had moved his family from Birkdale, Southport decades earlier. He had been a crew member since the formation of the lifeboat station at Fleetwood and was appointed as coxswain upon the retirement of Captain Wasey.

James Leadbetter was coxswain of the lifeboat *Edward Wasey* when on the 7th December, 1866 the lifeboat was launched to assist a vessel in distress West of Fleetwood. In storm conditions the Steam-tug *Wyre* with Captain William Swarbrick in command towed the lifeboat to the vicinity of the casualty and coxswain Leadbetter and his crew successfully save the thirteen crew members from the Norwegian barque *'Inga'*. In recognition of this service the grateful Norwegian ship owners commissioned a pastel depiction of the incident and presented this painting to Captain Swarbrick. This picture is still exhibited in the Fleetwood lifeboat station.

Lifeboat sustained storm damage in Lifeboat-house January 1863

Within three months of the *Edward Wasey* lifeboat being placed on station at Fleetwood and before she had been called out on active service a violent storm on 20th January, 1863 undermined the foundation of the boathouse almost washing it away. As the tide arose on Tuesday morning, it became evident that the lifeboat house, containing the new lifeboat, *Edward Wasey*, was in danger of being washed down. The lifeboat was mounted on its transporting carriage within the boathouse and the doors of the boathouse through which the lifeboat and carriage passed were on the seaward side. Due to the storm surge the high tide had risen considerably higher than predicted, with waves dashing furiously against them before anyone realised the situation. The lifeboat was floating still tethered to its carriage, making it impossible to take the boat out of the house, even if the boathouse doors could have been opened. Only by pulling down the rear gable end, with its access door facing the promenade, could the boat have been removed from the boathouse. Soon the crashing waves had undermined the foundation of the building; about one third of the walls on each side gave way and it became evident that the boathouse could not stand much longer. The coxswain James Leadbetter did not feel authorised to demolish the gable end of the building, although strong representations were made by onlookers encouraging him to take this step to save the new lifeboat and carriage from probable destruction. As the water continued to rise the lifeboat could be heard moving around in the boathouse on its trailer as the waves inside the boathouse pushed the floating boat and its launching carriage. People could hear crashing noises and knew the lifeboat must be damaged. Before long the boathouse roof fell in with a loud crash covering the boat with debris. A number of men instantly entered the ruins at considerable risk; succeeding in saving some of the apparatus but a great quantity of that was washed away by the sea and carried up the river. Ropes were made fast to the boat as the boathouse walls were about to tumble down and she was hauled around the corner of the building. All the spectators who could find a place for their hands on the ropes gave a pull to haul the boat and carriage higher up on the shore. She was landed on the walkway well above the high tide line.

The lifeboat had sustained considerable damage, with broken timbers in several places on her starboard side.

Horse drawn carriage launch of lifeboat

Within a day the lifeboat had been temporarily repaired but she required major repairs, at considerable expense, to restore her to her former condition. The boathouse was damaged beyond repair and to prevent a similar occurrence a new brick built lifeboat-house was erected in Pharos Place.

The first service call on the *Edward Wasey* lifeboat came on 29th October, 1863, to assist the schooner *Northern Lights*, of Preston, when she ran aground on Bernard Wharf. The lifeboat, under the command of coxswain James Leadbetter, was towed out by the steam-tug *Wyre*, skippered by Captain William Swarbrick. At the top of the channel the tow rope was slipped as they approached the casualty. It was a dark and stormy moonless night but the cries for help from those on board the *Northern Lights* could be heard above the violence of the storm. This helped the lifeboat crew to find the vessel that was aground in the breaking surf on the northern edge of Bernard Wharf. The lifeboat was manoeuvred into position under oar and approaching from the weather side the four crew were plucked to safety.

The storm continued overnight and the following day 30th October, 1863 the barque *Lillias*, of New Brunswick, dragged its anchors and grounded in the Lune Channel. Again the tug *Wyre*, with Captain Swarbrick and his crew, towed the lifeboat out to assist. On this occasion having slipped the lifeboat tow rope the tug found that they could get in close enough to the *Lillias* for 26 crew members to jump across onto the tug *Wyre*. The captain of the *Lillias* and two Mates decided to remain on board their stranded vessel and as the steam-tug *Wyre* departed to land their colleagues at Glasson Dock they asked the lifeboat to stand-by them in case there were problems as she re-floated. They secured a rope to the *Lillias* but at one point a large wave stuck the lifeboat, pushing it against the hull of the *Lillias*. Fortunately, no serious damage was done but the breaking waves made it difficult to maintain a position near to the *Lillias*. The strain on the rope had caused it to jam at the end tied to the vessel's hull and the lifeboat coxswain ordered the rope to be cut away to enable them to stand off at a further distance. Four hours after arriving at the *Lillias*, at around midnight, the lifeboat coxswain decided to leave the *Lillias* and return to station as the crew were exhausted and the barque would be aground for the next few hours. The lifeboat re-launched at daybreak to return to the Lillias and by this time the wind had moderated. The seas were still large from the previous storm and the lifeboat took some time to get back to the Lune Channel. When they returned to the *Lillias* they found that the three men had just been taken onto a steamer that was passing on its way to Glasson Dock and the *Lillias* had been abandoned.

James Turner coxswain 1870 – 1876

Lifeboat Coxswain James Turner

James Turner was a crew member of the lifeboat since 1859 at the formation of the lifeboat station and the delivery of the first lifeboat. He had been a crew member for over a decade and had participated in the medal service rescues with Captain Wasey. Having been involved in the rescue from the *Ann Mitchell* in 1860 he afterwards walked out across Pilling Sands to lead the Mate of the *Ann Mitchell*, John Barclay, to the upturned hull of that vessel to see if any bodies of the crew members could be located. James Turner gave evidence at the Coroners Inquest, held in the Bourne Arms hotel on the promenade at Knott End. He was appointed coxswain in 1870 and James retired in 1876.

George Doherty coxswain 1876 – 1878.

George Doherty was appointed coxswain 1876-1878. He was a Coastguard stationed at Fleetwood but within two years of his appointment as Coxswain of the lifeboat he was transferred to another Coastguard Station.

Record of Service Rendered by lifeboat *Edward Wasey* (1862-1879)

October 29th, 1863. Schooner *Northern Lights* of Preston. Aground on Bernard Wharf. Rescued the crew of four. Towed out by tug Wyre.

October 30th, 1863. Ship *Lillias* of New Brunswick. Aground in Lune Channel. Lifeboat towed out by tug Wyre. Tug got close enough for 26 crew to jump aboard. Captain and 2 Mates stayed on board until it refloated. Lifeboat stood by 3 hours.

October 20th, 1865. Brigantine *Highland Mary*. Aground on Bernard Wharf. Saved crew of 5.

December 7th, 1866. Barque *Inga* of Kragero.

April 1st, 1871. Soldier rescued from Beacon.

James Turner appointed Coxswain 1870-1876

George Doherty appointed coxswain 1876-1878 (he was then posted to another Coastguard Station).

Robert Wright appointed coxswain 1878.

September 18th, 1878. Barque *Charles Challoner*. Tug unable to hold barque and driven onto sandbank, just before midnight. Nineteen crew jumped onto tug before she swept away leaving one young boy on board. Lifeboat *Edward Wasey* was quickly launched and the crew succeeded in rescuing the boy.

August 29th, 1879. Schooner *Elizabeth Ellen Fisher*. Aground on Bernard Wharf sands. Stood-by vessel but filled with water. Lifeboat rescued crew of 4 men.

Lifeboat *'Child of Hale'* (1) (1879 – 1886)

The first Fleetwood lifeboat called *Child of Hale* arrived on station at Fleetwood September 1879. This lifeboat was 34 foot long, 8 foot 6 inches beam and self-righting. She was built at Woolfe boatyard Shadwell, London, at a cost of £363. The funding was a gift from Colonel William Blackburne of Leamington Spa who was a native of Hale, near Liverpool. The balance of the gift was used to fund a new lifeboat-house and slipway costing £450. This boathouse and slipway was constructed to the south of the present Knott-End ferry jetty.

Third Boathouse built South of present lifeboat pen

Record of Service Rendered by lifeboat *Child of Hale* (1879-1886)

February 16th, 1882. *'Venus'* of Helsingborg aground on Shell Wharf Bank. Rescued 9 men plus the Master's wife, young son and woman servant. Two days later the lifeboat helped refloat the vessel and brought into docks. Lifeboat towed by tug *'Relief'*.

January 27th 1883. Steamer *'Eden'* of West Hartlepool. Aground on Sunderland Bank. 25 people on board. Stood-by until refloated. One lifeboatman went onboard to pilot to Glasson.

August 10th, 1883. Norwegian Barque *'Jenny'* landed pilot from disabled barque. Later tug *Fylde* towed her into harbour.

October 24th, 1884. Barque *'Blackwell'* of London. Aground on North side of Lune Channel.

November 6th, 1886. Sloop *'Pennington'* of Liverpool. Rescued 2 crew. Vessel later became a total wreck.

November 26th, 1886. Brig *'Olga'* of Frederikstadt. In collision with barque *'Ruth Topping'* of Liverpool. 10 lifeboat-men put on *Ruth Topping* to help pump but *Ruth Topping's* nine crew plus Pilot were taken on board lifeboat. *Olga* then escorted into Fleetwood docks. *Ruth Topping* still afloat next day and lifeboat with extra crew brought her back to port.

Lifeboat *'Edith'* (1887-1894)

The lifeboat *'Edith'* arrived at the Fleetwood lifeboat station on 17th February, 1887. She was a 46 foot long vessel with 11 foot beam and self-righting. This lifeboat had been transferred from the New Brighton station where she had been on trials for three years. She was a gift from a Miss Carew of Shrewsbury and served at the Fleetwood station from 1887 to 1894, saving 19 lives. This boat was kept afloat on a river mooring and became Fleetwood's Number 2 lifeboat. Lifeboat *Edith* was withdrawn on March 17th 1894 and replaced by the 43 foot long by 12 foot 6 inch beam Watson Class non-self-righting lifeboat, named *Maude Pickup.*

Record of Service Rendered by lifeboat *Edith* (1887-1894)

October 31st, 1893. Steamer *'Odd'* of Norway. Fleetwood to Glasgow, in ballast, driven onto Bernard Wharf in Westerly Gale. Next day lifeboat *Edith* stood by until refloated.

November 17th, 1893. Schooner *'Theda'* of Caernarvon. Stranded on Sunderland Bank in dense fog. Lifeboat *Edith* found schooner full of water. Crew of seven, plus pilot rescued.

Lifeboat *'Child of Hale'* (2) (1887-1893)

On 31st March, 1887 the first *Child of Hale* lifeboat was replaced by a 37 foot long, 8 foot beam self-righting lifeboat. This lifeboat was the second vessel to be named *'Child of Hale'*. This boat had been built in 1887 by Woolfe and put in the reserve fleet. She had not been launched on active service before being assigned to the Fleetwood station. When placed at Fleetwood she was appropriated to the gift of Colonel Blackburne and named *'Child of Hale'*. She was on station for 6 years.

Lifeboat *Child of Hale (2)*

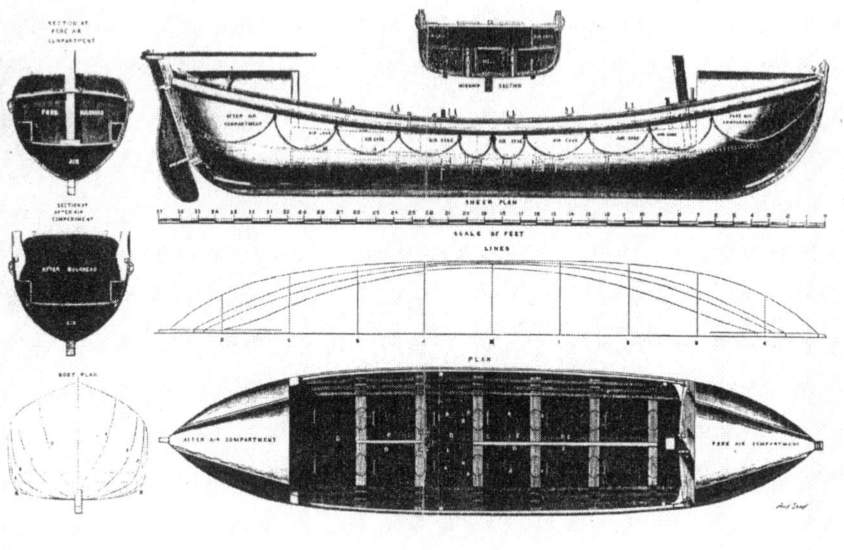

Plans of Lifeboat similar to second *Child of Hale*

Vessels *Labora* and *New Brunswick* wrecked November 7th, 1890

The closing months of the year 1890 were marked by a tale of disaster and woe at Fleetwood such as had not been known for many years. The following account is based on local newspaper reports of that time.

The storm that commenced on Thursday afternoon 6th November, 1890 was one of the most catastrophic that has ever visited the west coast of England. Captains of vessels entering the various ports in Morecambe Bay all stated that the gale was one of the worst they had seen for years. Seafaring men of experience in Fleetwood also felt that so fearful a storm had not been known on this part of the coast for a long time.

In Fleetwood, soon after midday on Thursday 6th November, 1890, it was evident that there was something unusual in the weather. A continuous downpour of rain was followed by strong southwesterly wind that within an hour rose to gale force. During Thursday evening the wind increased to hurricane force 12. The force and velocity of the wind was terrific. Frequently the strength of wind was so great that anyone walking along the streets was almost unable to maintain a footing. From early evening the wind strength had increased considerably and veered into the NorthWest. Many people had been woken up by the howling of the wind. For two hours hail and sleet unceasingly dashed against the window panes. The wind was still at hurricane force at about quarter past five on Friday morning when signals of distress were noticed from the area of Bernard Wharf in the form of rockets and the burning of tar barrels. The Lighthouse Keeper at once passed this information to the Coxswain of the lifeboat, who resided not far from the lifeboat-house. Coxswain Robert Wright at once fired his mortar in the street, in order to summon a crew. However, the task was made more difficult by the noise of the wind preventing many from hearing the explosive report. Only those men who lived in the direction in which the wind was blowing receiving the warning. At last, after the gun had been fired several times a crew was assembled, comprising the following:- Coxswain R. Wright and Messrs. Robert Fleming, William Fleming, Robert Ball, William Croft, J. W. Aspin, Thomas Wignall, Jeffrey Wright, Robert Wright, Thomas Wright, Fred Rimmer, John Leadbetter, William Wright, Albert Iddon, and Richard Wright. The *Child of Hale* was launched due to the rough sea causing exceptional difficulty in getting out to the second lifeboat *Edith* that was on a mooring in the river. The steam tug *Wardleys* towed the lifeboat out of the channel until they were clear of Wyre Light. In the meantime the storm continued to rage without abatement, and if anything it was worsening. Even near the Ferry Beach the water appeared one mass of seething waves, and ferry operations were cancelled on that day. The market traders could not get across the river, but the majority of the Over Wyre residents did not start on their journey down to the ferry slipway at Knott End, knowing the extreme state of the weather. Consequently, there was no market at Fleetwood. As daylight dawned upon this unusual scene many of the residents made their way to the hoarding near the Fleetwood Esplanade and onto the sea-front to watch what was happening out in the bay.

Steam tug *Wardleys* towing Child of Hale to barque *Labora*

The dim outline of the barque could be seen on Bernard Wharf, which afterwards turned out to be the stranded barque *Labora* of Egersund (Norway), bound for Fleetwood with logwood, skippered by Captain A. Scadberg, and owned by Mr. O. Puntervold. It was a barque of 682 tons, and was manned by the master and 12 men. The barque was valued at £3500, and the cargo at £3000. It was to this barque that the lifeboat made its way. The barque was at the North West point of Bernard Wharf, about a mile and a half north east of Wyre Light. From leaving the tug *Wardleys* at Wyre Light conditions were so bad it took a further hour in getting close to the barque. At last the lifeboat crew succeeded in getting a hawser from the barque. It then took another hour as exhausting work followed. On account of the high seas that prevailed, it would have been difficult to approach too near the *Labora*, so the coxswain of the lifeboat decided to take off the men by means of lifebuoy and lines. This was done and one by one the crew of the barque attached themselves to the buoy, dropping their bodies over the side and into the sea. One at a time they were hauled across into the lifeboat, the captain coming last.

As the lifeboat returned with the 13 men comprising the crew of the barque a cheer was raised by the spectators along the shore. At this time the wind was North North West, and it was still of severe gale force with driving rain. It was an hour and a half before high water.

The stranding of the barque was probably brought about by the fact that she drifted from her anchorage in Lune Deep, dragging her anchors with her. The rudder of the barque was gone, and it was plain to see she had encountered a heavy storm.

The coxswain reported that the lifeboat had behaved well in the extreme weather conditions. She had filled with water several times and was frequently on her beam ends. Whilst all this was taking place and as visibility had improved, another barque, which had not exhibited signals of distress according to the Merchant Shipping Act of 1873, was discernible further to the north-east of Bernard Wharf, about 3 miles from Wyre Light. This other barque transpired to be the *New Brunswick*, of New Brunswick, bound from Dalhousie to Glasson Dock with timber deals, skippered by Captain Hansen, and owned by S. W. Cock. She was in dire straits. Her masts had been cut away, and it was apparent she had stranded. The steam tug *Fylde* had gone out to her in the morning to inspect and reported that no signs of the crew were to be seen on her deck. This led to the supposition that the barque had been abandoned but the tug crew had found it difficult to tell whether there were any crew remaining on the barque, as the spray had been almost blinding in intensity. Telegrams had been dispatched to different ports around Morecambe Bay, enquiring whether the crew had landed, but no information could be obtained. Glasson Dock reported a small boat on the sands, and it was concluded the crew had taken to the boat, and were lost. Many conjectures were made but the uncertainty of everything lead to a consultation taking place about 3 o'clock in the afternoon between Captain Jackson (chairman of the lifeboat committee), Coxswain Wright, and the others, the result of which it was determined to call the lifeboat crew together. The steam tug *Wardley's* again held herself in readiness, and it was decided on this occasion to take out the *Edith* lifeboat that was anchored in her usual place at the opposite side of the Wyre. There was a slight difference in the lifeboat crew this time. Messrs. Robert Ball and William Croft did not go with the *Edith* lifeboat and Messrs. Gilbert Ball, James Helm, and Robert Wright, Jr., went out the second time, but did not go with the *Child of Hale*. The gale had now somewhat subsided, but was still moderately severe, with heavy seas at the mouth of the river near Wyre Light.

Lifeboat *Edith* approaching barque *New Brunswick*

On arrival at the *New Brunswick* a considerable amount of debris was found floating about her, which made it difficult for the lifeboat to approach. After some difficulty rowing towards her the crew of the *Edith* succeeded in getting to leeward of the barque and the whole of the barque's crew, comprising 11 men who had been sheltering below deck, came up onto the deck one by one. Although this had surprised the lifeboat crew to find people still on board it was quickly decided how an attempt would be made to take them off the stricken vessel. Once the lifeboat had been placed alongside this task was not quite so difficult as in the case of the *Labora*, the violence of the storm having subsided. There was a short choppy sea, and the tide was about two hours flood. It is supposed that the *New Brunswick* dragged her anchor and went aground. She was valued at £2,500; the cargo at £1,000. The master of the barque stated afterwards that they stranded about 5.00 a.m. that morning and that he hoisted a piece of canvas in the rigging as a signal of distress but the masts then came down. This made a total of 24 lives rescued by the Fleetwood lifeboats on Friday 7th November. During this storm twenty five lifeboats around the UK, belonging to the Royal National Lifeboat Institution, had been launched to assist vessels in distress. The total number of lives saved by them was 96, and of these 24 of those were rescued by the Fleetwood lifeboat. The gallantry displayed by the crews of the Fleetwood lifeboats and also of the steam tugs taking part in these rescues was praised in the local newspapers. All the rescues were effected without any mishap and the crew on each occasion displayed the greatest bravery and gallantry. It should also be added that the services of the steam tugs are voluntary and great praise is due to the manner in which the steam tug *Wardleys* was placed at the services of the lifeboat. On the second occasion the tugs stood by for two hours in the rough seas. The journeys of the tugs were perilous and they were tossed around in the rough seas. Capt. Blundell of the *Wardleys*, along with chief engineer T. Gibson and their crew were praised for assisting in the rescue. The *Fylde* was also involved in giving what assistance she could by going out and trying to gain some knowledge of the *New Brunswick*. The assistance of the steam-tugs had not been generally recognised in any practical degree, yet their services were invaluable. The rescued men were at once provided with comfortable accommodation in the town on their return. Many of the men were in an exhausted state. On Sunday lots of people visited the *Labora* either by walking over the sands at low tide, or by rowing down the channel the distance, and then walking the remainder. The same day the tugs *Wardleys* and *Fylde* towed the *New Brunswick's* hull into Glasson Dock.

Anecdotally, one of the men from the *Labora* did something that the newspapers recorded from this incident. When he had been dragged through the surging waters into the lifeboat, whilst still in the water he looked around at the lifeboatmen and laconically remarked "good morning" as he was hauled alongside. It was reported that 'probably it was not because the rescued man lacked gratitude in the least, but because he was carried away by excitement that he simply delivered himself of the first words which occurred to him'. The captain of the

Labora saw that the weaker and fatigued members of the crew went into the lifeboat first. In one case stimulants had to be administered before the crewman would leave the stricken vessel. The captain had the

Lifeboat crew of *Child of Hale (2)*

presence of mind to jump off with a large clasp knife between his teeth so that he could cut the ropes attached to the ship with which he might have become entangled. The rescued crew members were received by Mr. G. Scott, and then placed under the care of Mr. J. N. Ward, Norwegian vice consul. Through the generosity of Mr James Richardson, of Poulton, who watched the landing of the first crew, the shipwrecked crew, as well as the crew of the lifeboat, were supplied with refreshments at the Fleetwood station refreshment rooms. The rescued men were sent home to Norway, on Tuesday, by Mr. Ward.

The newspapers reported 'Owing to the careful and judicious way in which the lifeboats were handled they received little or no damage. On leaving the first wreck Coxswain Wright was compelled to cut his cable, thus losing his anchor and part of his cable. On the second trip the new wire cable came in very useful, and stood the wear and tear against a large amount of wreckage much better than the Manilla one could possibly have done, while at the same time it was more easily worked, thus proving Coxswain Wright's contention that these are the best cables for lifeboats.'

Robert Wright coxswain 1878 – 1895.

Coxswain Robert Wright had succeeded George Doherty when he was transferred to another station within the Coastguard Service. He was becoming elderly by the time of the *Labora* and *New Brunswick* incidents but he had a life time's experience of the sea and was described as a cool, clearheaded man. He had been coxswain for around 12 years at this time and prior to that time he frequently was one of the lifeboat crew. Many lives had been saved during his period of service. In 1885 he had received a presentation of opera glasses (binoculars) from the institution for his lifeboat labours. The service to the *Labora* and *New Brunswick* on the part of the Fleetwood lifeboat had been outstanding. As well as coxswain Robert Wright, second coxswain Robert Fleming, and every man taking part were congratulated upon their exertions.

When he retired in October 1895 he had completed 36 years in the lifeboat service, the last 17 years as coxswain and was awarded a second Silver Medal to mark his remarkable contribution. It was calculated that 200 people owed their lives to him and his men.

His planned retirement in October 1895 was sadly affected by the loss of his son James Wright, who was also a member of the lifeboat crew. His son-in-law Robert Fleming, of North Church Street, was second coxswain of the lifeboat. Both were lost on the same night in a 'Great Gale' on the 1st and 2nd of October, 1895. This gale caused a disaster for the town of Fleetwood where many families were plunged into grief, mourning the loss of their menfolk when their fishing boats were caught out by the severe weather and lost at sea. A disaster fund was set up across the whole area to assist families. For weeks each tide brought bodies back to the shore and the whole town was affected by the scale of loss of friends and relatives. Robert Fleming was skipper of their fishing smack *Schoolgirl* and James was the Mate when it was overwhelmed by the bad weather. Later in the same month Coxswain Wright's 18 year old grandson Robert Wright of East Street, was lost at sea in a separate storm when the barque *Highland Home*, on passage from Fleetwood to London, foundered with the loss of all the crew. The retirement presentations to Robert Wright were appropriately subdued due to the recent bereavement in such terrible circumstances. The newspaper described Coxswain Robert Wright as 'A Storm Warrior' who was held in high esteem by his fellow townsfolk and wedded to the lifeboat service. Tributes described him as honest, unassuming, ready at the call of duty, unflinching, strong and resourceful in the hour of danger.

Robert Wright and his wife Sarah had nine children and he died at the age of 72 in 1902.

A disaster off Walney Island - loss of five lives.

However, the above incidents were eclipsed by other events on the same day. On Friday night 7th November, 1890 the residents of Fleetwood unexpectedly heard of a disaster with one of the fishing smacks - the *Osprey* owned by Mr George Ormerod, of Southport - whilst endeavouring to render assistance to the crew of a sinking schooner, a mile or two off Walney Island. It appears that the schooner was probably the same which was passed by Captain Rodger, of the *Laurel,* one of the Lavid line of steamers running from Londonderry to Morecambe. Captain Rodger was off the approaches to Morecambe Bay early on the Friday morning, but was forced by the weather conditions to beat back to Ramsey Bay. On the way a clipper-rigged schooner was noticed to be in distress towards the Cumbrian coast, off Barrow-in-Furness, but they were unable to render assistance in the extreme weather and on a lee shore.

Alarming reports of this disaster reached Fleetwood about 7 o'clock in the evening. About that time the scene at the fish warehouse was almost indescribable. Fishermens' wives and children were enquiring whether such-and-such a fishing smack had arrived and when they received a reply in the negative their screams testified to their anguish. Sometimes the reply would be of a more reassuring character and then some such exclamation as 'Thank God' would it be heard. It was indeed a scene of great anguish. When James Fogg, the skipper of the

Osprey, which was formerly a yacht, arrived it was evident from his horror-stricken appearance that he had startling news to convey.

He was coming in from sea on that afternoon with, besides himself, three men and the 'cook', the latter being the name given to the ship's boy. Whilst off Barrow-in-Furness an unknown schooner was seen to be indicating signals of distress, with the men on the schooner shouting to be taken on board the fishing smack. Without hesitation James Fogg ordered his rowing punt to be launched and with three crew members on-board it they set out to attempt a rescue. The schooners crew were seen to be climbing into the rigging and their plight was pitiable. The *Osprey* was about 50 yards from the schooner at that time, and the punt succeeded in getting three men off the schooner. All went well until the punt containing the six men had almost returned to the smack when a

The *Osprey's* boat sinks on the return journey

large wave struck the punt causing it to capsize, throwing all the occupants into the rough seas. Breaking waves were all around them but Fogg managed to throw a lifebuoy and rescued one of his own crew, named George Wilkinson.

Two crew members from the *Osprey*, along with all three men from the Schooner were drowned. All efforts to save them being to no avail, on account of the high seas and the storm conditions. Three men from the schooner were unknown. The other two men who were drowned, and who formed part of the crew of the *Osprey*, were single men, residing in Fleetwood. Their names were James Abram and George Greenall. It was about half-past-four in the afternoon when Fogg, having only the assistance of the boy headed for Fleetwood, some nine miles South across Morecambe Bay. They reached Fleetwood that evening in an exhausted state, the main sail was split from top to bottom and they had to make headway with the foresail as best they could. The name of the 'cook' was John Robert Tomlinson. The skipper, James Fogg, explained to the newspaper reporter using his own language, that they were overtaken by the storm on Thursday afternoon, about one p.m., 'that came like the shot out of a gun'.

The schooner's crew had managed to cling to the capsized boat. Greenall was seen swimming on an oar, but Abram was carried off at once. What made the affair more painful for their friends was that Abram was a member of the Salvation Army at Fleetwood and only the previous Sunday was speaking on the uncertainty when death might occur, and the need for preparedness. On Sunday the congregations of local churches were told of the sad event. Throughout the Fylde great sympathy was expressed for the relatives of the fishermen who were drowned.

On Saturday 8th November, 1890 it was reported that a schooner had gone ashore near Cleveleys about midnight on Friday night, with no signs of life on board. She proved to be the *Jean Campbell* of Wigtown, with a cargo of coal, and is was supposed she was the same schooner from which the Fleetwood fishermen attempted to rescue the crew on Friday afternoon. An examination of the wreck showed that she had driven stern on, and at the time there was no crew aboard. The cargo of coal was insured by the Maritime Insurance Company, Liverpool, and on Monday afternoon carts were engaged in discharging the coal at low-water with the object of lightening the vessel (as well as saving the coal), in order to float her off. The schooner was owned by Messrs. McCowan, of Balbriggan, near Dublin. It was later confirmed that she was the same schooner the *Osprey* encountered.

Monument in Euston Park Fleetwood

The three crew of the '*Jean Campbell*' were drowned along with James Abram and George Greenall from the *Osprey*. The only survivor was George Wilkinson, who had been hauled to safety by James Fogg and the fishing smack *Osprey's* cook. For their courageous efforts to save the crew of the '*Jean Campbell*', James Fogg and George Wilkinson were each awarded a Silver Medal by the R.N.L.I.

A fund was set-up locally for the dependents of James Abram and George Greenall.

To commemorate this incident a Monument to the gallantry of all those involved was erected in the ornamental gardens in the Euston Park.

Record of Service Rendered by lifeboat *Child of Hale (2)* (1887-1893)

August 22nd 1889. - *S.S. Britannia.* No effective service. At sea ten and a half hours in violent seas and full NW gale.

November 7th 1890. Barque *Labora* of Egursund.. Distress signals were spotted on Bernard Wharf. At 06.05 hrs the Child of Hale launched – Cox. Robert Wright. They set up a breeches buoy and rescued the crew of 13 persons.

November 7th 1890. Shortly after the crew were landed from the *Labora* incident, the Number 2 lifeboat *Edith* slipped her mooring around 15.00 hrs to assist the vessel *New Brunswick* with a crew of 11 on board. She had lost all her masts. Huge seas were sweeping clean over her. Coxswain Wright rescued the whole crew of eleven.

November 7th 1890. On the same day as the *Labora* and *New Brunswick* rescues the *Osprey - Jean Campbell* incident took place that is commemorated by a monument in Euston Park.

December 11th 1890. A Silver medal was awarded to Coxswain Robert Wright in recognition of many years of dedicated service.

December 14th, 1891. Fishing Smack *'Superb'* reported in difficulty, but help of lifeboat was ultimately not required.

In 1893 the Railway Company needed the lifeboat-house site that had been in position since 1879 for harbour extensions. A new lifeboat-house was built that was large enough to accommodate the larger Number 2 lifeboat, just West of the Lower Lighthouse.

Later that year the second *'Child of Hale' (2)* lifeboat was withdrawn and the station reverted to one lifeboat.

3 LIFEBOAT '*MAUDE PICKUP*' (1894-1930)

The lifeboat *Maude Pickup* was a 43 foot long by twelve foot six inch beam non-self-righting lifeboat. She was gifted from the legacy of the late Mr. James Pickup of Southport. During the thirty six years at the Fleetwood lifeboat station she was involved in many dramatic rescues.

Maude Pickup lifeboat painting by Ken Frost

For generations the crews of lifeboats around the British coast were drawn from the ranks of local inshore fishermen. They were hardy souls who spent long hours outside in all weathers. They knew the sea in all its moods and the geography of the area near their base. The lifeboat was usually needed in rough weather and that meant the fishermen would be port-bound from their fishing operations and available for duty risking their lives to help others.

Fleetwood was no exception. As the infant town developed, fishermen from the Marshside area near Southport - villages including Banks and Hesketh Bank re-located themselves in Fleetwood, alongside a few local men already working the nets and lines.

Their main catch was the shrimp but when this declined white fish took over. Originally, the Southport men were unhappy about the shrimp prices they had been getting at home. Coming to Fleetwood must have been akin to the pioneers who settled the American West but they came and quickly established themselves and their families in the growing Fleetwood community. Many had a strong link to the Mount Methodist church.

And so it was that names like Wright and Leadbetter began to appear in the records of Fleetwood RNLI.

One was Robert Wright who had been a crew member since the station was founded in 1859. He was appointed Coxswain in 1878 and served for 17 years during which time he was in charge during some spectacular rescues in very bad weather.

None were worse than the November day in 1890 when an exceptionally violent storm lashed the Lancashire coast. It became known as the Great Gale. Robert Wright and his men went out twice in one day to rescue 13 men from one wreck and 11 from another.

Both ships were loaded with timber bound for Fleetwood and belonged to Norwegian owners. The government of that country gave the Fleetwood lifeboatmen £10 each in recognition of their lifesaving feat.

At the same time, Fleetwood fishermen James Abram and George Greenall lost their lives during a separate rescue mission as they struggled home through the storm as crewmen in the fishing craft Osprey. Her skipper, James Fogg together with George Wilkinson – the only survivor of the three crewmen who rowed out from the *Osprey* to attempt to rescue the crew of the *Jean Campbell* – were awarded Silver Medals by the RNLI and so was Coxswain Robert Wright.

On another occasion the RNLI presented him with a pair of binoculars after service to a steamship aground in rough seas which safely reached port after being refloated.

A fund was established in Fleetwood for the families of James Abram and George Greenall and a monument to them was placed in the Euston Park within sight of the sea that claimed their lives.

Described as a person of 'manly bearing and genial disposition' Robert

Wright was famed as a lifeboat-man well beyond the boundaries of his home town.

David Leadbetter coxswain 1895 - 1906

Robert Wright was succeeded by the bearer of another famous Fleetwood name – David Leadbetter.

Lifeboat Coxswain David Leadbetter

He started work as a boy with his father in the fishing boat Eagle (census data shows him working as a fisherman at the age of 12 years) and he was only 18 when he was awarded his Skipper's Certificate and then commanded several Fleetwood-based smacks. These sail-powered vessels had a crew of three or four and used the wind and tide to drag a trawl net across the seabed on fishing grounds around the eastern Irish Sea.

They stayed at sea for days at a time and were the fore-runners of the steam-powered trawlers which turned Fleetwood into the UK's third biggest fishing port.

Fleetwood was also the base for some large sailing yachts owned by wealthy Lancashire businessmen. Each summer they recruited local fishermen to act as skippers and crew members and David Leadbetter commanded such craft. One was *Olivia* owned by Mr S L Clegg of the Royal Mersey Yacht Club.

In the winter David went fishing in a prawner – much smaller than a smack and remaining at sea for 12 or 24 hours with two men onboard.

Married with five children, David Leadbetter lived in the heart of old Fleetwood – in Pharos Street a few minutes walk from the lifeboat station. This was the case with most of the crew for generations.

What made David Leadbetter unique among Fleetwood Coxswains was his additional role in talking about the work of the RNLI in many towns and cities around the country as a public speaker. The Institution has always relied on the generosity of the public and has never wanted to be part of a government-backed organisation. He must have made a convincing orator for he spoke from real experience but many modern-day lifeboatmen would find it a daunting task to speak on a public platform.

Coxswain Leadbetter's most noteworthy feat was in June, 1897 when three ships were driven aground on Pilling Sands in a heavy gale. A total of 18 seafarers were saved in one journey by the lifeboat.

During David Leadbetter's time as Coxswain between 1894 and 1909, no fewer than 72 lives were saved by the Fleetwood crews. He had received a gold watch and binoculars in recognition of his work.

David Leadbetter died from a heart condition at the age of 52.

Wednesday June 16th, 1897. *Svalen, Louise* and *Zillah*

The day of Wednesday 16th June, 1897 was an eventful day for Fleetwood Lifeboat when no less than 18 lives were saved from three vessels in difficult and hazardous conditions. Overnight the Fylde coast had been battered by an unusually severe Summer storm, the same one that had wrecked Nelson's former flagship *Foudroyant* earlier that day along the Blackpool shore, near to North Pier.

Steam Lighter *Zillah*

At 9.00 p.m. on Tuesday 15th June, 1897, the steam lighter *Zillah* had left Raynes Jetty at Llanddulas in Colwyn Bay, North Wales, where for the previous 3 days they had loaded a cargo of limestone. Within an hour and once clear of the coast the crew had supper as they proceeded North Eastwards at a steady seven knots towards their destination port of Fleetwood, a distance of around 50 miles. The *Zillah*, a small steamer belonging to the Steam Shipping Co. of Warrington, had a full cargo of limestone destined for the United Alkali Company on the River Wyre. Soon after supper and from around 10.00 p.m. the weather deteriorated and continued to worsen throughout the night.

Besides Captain Skellen the ship's master, there were on board, the Mate Hulse; the Engineer Sprowsen; Fireman Gardy; and the Cook Harrison. Overnight the seas continued to build and with the West by Southerly wind blowing on their port quarter the *Zillah* was rolling considerably. Around 2.00 a.m. the lookout picked up the distant loom of Morecambe Bay Lightship and the weather was getting worse. Later, as dawn was breaking, they passed around five miles East of the lightship heading towards the Lune Light vessel. The weather was still poor, with South-Westerly gale force winds and progress was only slow as the engineers were finding that with the extreme rolling motion it was becoming difficult to continue to feed the coal-fired boiler to maintain any good head of steam. Before breakfast time the cook found it impossible to use the galley stove so they didn't have any hot drink or food throughout the fourteen hours of their voyage.

The *Zillah* passed Lune Light vessel about 6.00 a.m., around low water, and altered course towards Wyre Light. When she arrived off Fleetwood, the wind was 'boisterous', to use the captain's own phrase, and was still blowing at gale force from a West by South direction. The *Zillah* arrived off Fleetwood Fairway No. 1 buoy about seven o' clock in the morning but prior to that time she had been having a heavy time of it with the strong wind and high breaking seas. The increasing tidal flood current caused the vessel to experience difficulty in getting into the Fleetwood channel. In spite of the best endeavours of the engineers to maintain boiler steam pressure, she was drifting E. by N. in the direction of the Heysham channel unable to make headway over the ground due to the strong wind and adverse tidal current.

As the morning advanced the wind increased to a severe gale and with reduced boiler steam pressure their vessel was unable to make any progress towards Fleetwood. Around 10.30 a.m. the harbour tug *Fylde* was in their vicinity. As the tug approached they hailed her for assistance and the *Zillah* was taken in tow by the tug *Fylde*. For about an hour the two vessels crept towards the Wyre channel, making only slow progress. Unfortunately, through the stress of the weather, having entered the River Wyre around 11.30 a.m., as the tug *Fylde* approached No. 4 buoy with the *Zillah* in tow the wind and tide pushed the pair of vessels eastwards across the Fleetwood channel and although the *Fylde* managed to clear No 4 buoy the tow-rope connecting *Zillah* became fouled around the buoy. In order to get clear it was necessary for the *Fylde* to cast off from the *Zillah*. The tow rope unfortunately then became entangled in the *Fylde's* propeller. Unable to clear it from the propeller shaft the tug *Fylde* limped back to port at slow speed, having been forced to abandon the *Zillah* and its crew.

Earlier that morning and before the incident with the *Zillah* and tug *Fylde* had taken place; at Fleetwood quite a number of vessels were seen to be in danger in the vicinity of Pilling Sands. Telegraph reports had also been received from Lancaster, along with other reports from Glasson and Cockerham asking for assistance from the lifeboat for vessels in difficulties on the eastern shore of Morecambe Bay. About the same time distress signals were seen from a barque northeast of Fleetwood. Soon after 8.00 a.m. the lifeboat maroons were fired to summon the crew. Within quarter of an hour the crew were assembled at the life-boathouse that was located West of the Lower lighthouse, and the boat was run out on the slipway in preparation for launching. At about nine o'clock when the tug was available, the lifeboat, *Maude Pickup*, under the command of Coxswain David Leadbetter, was launched to assist the storm-tossed vessels. It was the first time in three years that the lifeboat had been launched on active service and apart from lifeboat practice launches it was the first time David Leadbetter, who had been a long-time crew member, had been on a rescue call as coxswain. The lifeboat was taken in tow by Captain Brodie of the steam tug *Brock* and their progress was watched by crowds of anxious spectators gathered along the promenade at various points where they clustered together to shelter from the strong winds. The flood-tide surged down the channel and the waves were flicked white by the wind. When the tug and lifeboat were clear of the Wyre channel the tug *Brock* released the *Maude Pickup* and sails were set on the lifeboat in readiness to head East into the Glasson Channel. The wind was SouthWest at gale force and the lifeboat was able to make good progress with the wind giving her a broad reach.

The vessel that the *Maude Pickup* lifeboat headed for appeared to be aground on the far side of Bernard Wharf about midway between the Pilling coast and the Wyre Light and some two miles from the shore. She was believed to be the barque, *Svalen* of Tvedestrand in Norway, bound to Glasson Dock from Halifax, Nova Scotia, with a cargo of timber and had been lying at anchor in the Lune Deeps for nearly a fortnight, waiting for the high Spring tides. Still further to the west, closer to Wyre Light, and now apparently aground was the Liverpool flag barque, *William and Ann*, but it was known that the crew – Captain Lee and two men – had been brought ashore earlier in the day on a harbour tug, so no action was to be taken.

There was a full gale blowing and a nasty sea running as the lifeboat headed directly for the *Svalen*, finding her further up the Glasson Channel than she had appeared previously. She was ashore on Sunderland Point, full of water and with seas was breaking over her. Her stern post was broken, her rudder knocked off and the main mast was down. Another mast fell as the lifeboat was approaching her and the shrouds and rigging went overboard. Coxswain Leadbetter said "I never saw a ship in greater strait'". The waves were much worse on the sands than in deeper water. Large waves were breaking right over the barques hull and sweeping across its superstructure. From the lifeboat they could see men crouched, half dead with cold and exposure. Even if the barque didn't soon completely break up those men clinging to the stern cabin deck-house could not have endured much more. She had three men on board, that were later found to be the mate, the steward, and the carpenter. Captain Svenson and the rest of the crew had gone ashore in the ship's boat the day before and were unable to get back on board when the weather suddenly deteriorated.

The lifeboat coxswain had difficulty in getting close to the *Svalen's* hull, owing to the wreckage strewn around the hull and the high breaking seas. The coxswain positioned the lifeboat so they could anchor and veer down on the *Svalen* but the lifeboat's anchor fouled the barque's cable and they had to cut away from it. At first the coxswain had little hope of saving the men, but they did achieve it. The only way they could get the men off was by hauling them through some fifty feet of water, the men jumping off the stern of the barque attached to the line and the lifeboat crewmen pulling them on board the lifeboat. The steward came first, then the carpenter, followed by the mate. The mate saw that the other two were properly lashed to the rope and then when it came to his own turn, after fixing the around his body, he sprang into the sea and was reported to have 'swam in splendid style' to the lifeboat. The condition of one older man – the carpenter – was pitiful. He was trembling from head to foot as he was pulled up into the lifeboat and some of the lifeboat crew actually pulled off their own clothes to put on this man. The other two rescued men were completely exhausted, and it occurred to Coxswain Leadbetter that on future occasions they would have to provide something in the way of a restorative. The barque *Svalen* became a total wreck and Coxswain Leadbetter was reported as stating 'we had the greatest difficulty of all in getting the men off her. Never in my experience on the lifeboat have I had a harder job than the one we had in rescuing these three men. We were no less than 2 hours before we succeeded in getting them on board the lifeboat'.

Away to the South-East of the River Lune channel another barque could be seen to have been driven ashore. On leaving the wrecked hull of the *Svalen* the lifeboat then proceeded in a south-easterly direction, to the barque *Louise* that was lying on the south side of Glasson channel. She had a crew of nine (Captain Anderson, master), and there was also on board Pilot Gerrard, of Fleetwood. The lifeboat's sails were lowered as they approached the *Louise* and they rowed the lifeboat alongside. There was just enough water to get under the lee side with some shelter from the barques hull and there was no difficulty whatever in getting the crew off her even though the wind was still gale force. Coxswain Leadbetter said "We never even had to anchor due to the way the barque's hull was" and the lifeboat was taken in under the stern. The men were all gathered on the port quarter poop when the lifeboat closed in and they simply jumped off the stern into the lifeboat. Pilot Gerrard had his foot injured as he fell heavily into the lifeboat but he was able to stand and move around. When the lifeboat left the *Louise* with the survivors on-board Pilot Gerrard looked at his watch and in discussion with coxswain Leadbetter they both gauged that they would have enough water to cross Pilling Sands and make straight for Fleetwood harbour.

Meanwhile, on the Fleetwood Promenade as the lifeboat was seen by the spectators to sail further and further away towards Sunderland Shoulder the attention of the observers was attracted to the movements of the tug *Fylde*, which could be seen in the vicinity of Wyre Light to be heading towards Fleetwood with a steam lighter in tow. Shortly afterwards, to the astonishment of those on shore viewing through telescopes, it was evident that the vessels had parted company, for while the tug continued to make way, though slowly, the steam lighter *Zillah* drifted in to the shallows and towards the sandbanks on the eastern side of the Fleetwood channel. As the anxious minutes passed, it became more evident that the steam lighter – the *Zillah* as she proved to be – was sinking. Without sufficient steam pressure to maintain any speed she began to drift eastwards. Her condition soon became hopeless and the vessel was swept by every wave. Her boiler fires were in a very short time extinquished by water entering the ventilation cowls and shortly afterwards she struck the sandbank of Bernard Wharf. There she remained, pounding on the sandbank with every minute seeing the waves mount higher and higher as the tide came in. The crew took to the rigging – or rather the captain and mate took to the rigging, the engineer and fireman with great difficulty managed to get towards the top of the funnel, and the cook found a perilous footing on the top of the ventilator. While in this terrible position, the engineer had the misfortune to lose his grip and fall to the bottom of the funnel, but although severely hurt he was able, with the assistance of the fireman, to regain his position although he was covered from head to foot with greasy soot from the lining of the funnel.

From the Fleetwood shore some two miles away and at about mid-day, *Zillah* was seen to settle down on the sea-bed. Her crew were seen clambering up the rigging, or any point of safety they could reach. Although the vessel was believed to be in not more than 12 feet of water waves were breaking right over her hull. As the tide was just about at its height at noon it was hoped she would be able to withstand the gale. Every sea swept her from stem to stern, and it was an awful sight to see the seamen exposed to the driving sea. With great difficulty the crew tried to find places to cling to above the breaking seas. One man perched actually on the top of the funnel, and soon he was joined by a comrade in this awful position; others had climbed the foremast. From their elevated post, they saw the lifeboat leave the *Svalen* with the survivors on board and also saw her come away equally successfully from the *Louise*. As the lifeboat headed westward across Pilling Sands frantic efforts were made by the *Zillah's* crew to attract the lifeboat crew to their plight. They were relieved when they saw the lifeboat alter course to turn its bow towards them.

As the *Maude Pickup* was beating south-westwards on the wind returning towards the Fleetwood channel, Coxswain Leadbetter suddenly stiffened as his sharp experienced eyes saw a blurred shape in the distance that he knew to be a ship that was probably in distress. He yelled against the clamour of the storm to 'Toby' Wright, his bowman and one of his most experienced hands, pointing over on the starboard bow. 'Toby' and most of the crew turned to peer too in that direction, one by one confirming what the coxswain had seen.

As they proceeded across the sands and got closer to the vessel they could see her submerged hull and saw the men on board making signals from the mast and funnel top. They had to tack a few times to beat across towards her.

Rescuing the crew from the steamer *Zillah*

When they were within half a mile they could clearly see the masts and funnel, realising that a vessel had sunk. On their arrival Coxswain Leadbetter quickly assessed the situation and ran the lifeboat at the foremast and bow of the *Zillah* and rescued the captain and mate from the rigging with little trouble. Due to the obstruction of the *Zillah's* superstructure it was difficult to get in close to the funnel and the coxswain decided to repeat the procedure successfully undertaken earlier at the barque *Svalen.* The sails were lowered and the lifeboat, under oar, was positioned off the port quarter of the submerged hull. Waiting for his opportunity the coxswain then ordered the lifeboat to be rowed in close enough to throw a line across to the funnel but not close enough for the lifeboat to collide with the superstructure. When the line was secured to the funnel the three men were hauled, one at a time, through the sea by means of the line, a distance of 30 yards or so. The lifeboat had to be constantly manoeuvred under oars before they got the last of them on board and were then able to get the sails up and head for Fleetwood.

From the shore the spectators watching the *Maude Pickup* were concerned for those on board the sunken vessel. They saw the lifeboat alter course to gradually make her way towards the steam lighter. Precisely at twelve minutes to one o' clock, the lifeboat was seen to be alongside the *Zillah*, or as near as she could get, and then after a further series of manoeuvres, lines were thrown out and one by one the five men of the *Zillah* were taken on board the lifeboat. Thereafter, smart seamanship and the strong wind soon brought the lifeboat back to the shore, where they tied up at the Fleetwood ferry slip to land the survivors. Cheers went up from the crowded quays as all eighteen men stepped ashore, some in bedraggled and exhausted condition.

The gallant crew of the *Maude Pickup* had brought everyone there had been on board the three vessels, without any loss of life. They had saved no fewer than 18 lives, namely, five men from the *Zillah*, three from the *Svalen*, and nine from the *Louise* plus pilot Gerrard. When Captain Skellen was landed, he was bleeding from a severe wound on the forehead. He said it had been caused by his being thrown against the foremast on board his vessel. He had been in a shipwreck before, but he stated: "I have never been in such a bad mess before." Regarding the rescuers, he was full of praise, and, he specifically stated that the *Maude Pickup* "was handled magnificently by the coxswain and crew." One of the survivors, on reaching land simply collapsed, overcome by the relief of reaching safety after the ordeal they had faced.

The news spread like wildfire throughout the town and people expressed their tremendous joy to know that the work of rescue, accomplished in the face of one of the worst storms in recent years had been effected so smartly, efficiently, and heroically.

Following their return David Leadbetter stood quietly at the stern of the *Maude Pickup*, his elbow resting on the gunwale, his forearm supporting his head as a feeling of exhaustion came upon him. He quietly reflected on the events of that day and the fact that 18 people had been saved. When the press reporter approached him he snapped out of the dazed state that had temporarily come upon him. Responding to the questions the Coxswain could not praise the lifeboat too much, stating: "I only wish you will praise her all you can, and that there will soon be more non-capsizable boats. This is the best test we have ever had, and the boat could not have done better". The coxswain while praising his boat, did not forget to praise – and deservedly so his gallant lifeboat crew, each of whom he said had done his share in the hard day's work.

The reception given to the rescuers and rescued was in the nature of an ovation, and to the lifeboat crew was some small indication of the gratitude felt towards them for their noble work. Such gallant deeds, however, are not to be measured by words or plaudits. The proud satisfaction remains within Fleetwood that her men, ever ready at the call of duty, had again displayed the heroism that without a boast places its life at the disposal of its fellows, in the knowledge that it has not been done in vain. On this occasion eighteen lives were saved through their noble work.

There were in total fifteen crew on board the Fleetwood lifeboat *Maude Pickup*, and the Fleetwood Times newspaper expressed their genuine pleasure in giving the names of the heroes. They were:- David Leadbetter (coxswain), J.R. Leadbetter (second coxswain), Richard Wright (bowman), Matthew Boardman, John Salthouse, Charles Hughes, John Leadbetter, Thomas Leadbetter, Matthew Cowell, Tom Percy, John Wright, Fred Bettess, L. Bond, Nicholas Abraham, and J. Roskell. They added that the signaller was John Salthouse. The newspaper published in tribute a photograph of the Fleetwood Lifeboat crew in a special supplement.

Photograph of Fleetwood lifeboat crew in commemorative issue of Fleetwood Times following rescues of 16th June, 1897

Fleetwood lifeboat crew 1897 Front row: Left to right – Tom Percy, Nicholas Abram, 'Judy' Wright, Tom Leadbetter. Second row: Left to right – Joseph Leadbetter, Bowman 'Toby' Wright, Coxswain David Leadbetter, Second Coxswain John Robert Leadbetter, Dick Leadbetter. Third row: - Jim Roskell, John Salthouse, Charley Hughes, Matt Boardman, F. Bettess, Matt Cowell and Lawrence Bond.

20th February, 1906 - Old Hunter and Maggie Kelso

The vagaries of weather were a constant challenge to any skipper of a sailing collier as the ships of this trade were chosen, not for speed but for the amount of coal they could carry as cargo.

The schooner *Old Hunter*, owned by Messrs. James Fisher and Sons of Barrow in Furness was almost thirty years old, having been built at Berwick by Gowan in 1877. She was of wooden construction with copper fastenings and registered as 79 tons, 81 foot length, 21 foot beam and drawing 10 foot draught. *Old Hunter* had spent the previous week in Liverpool loading a full cargo of coal for shipment to Mevagissey in Cornwall. By Friday evening (16th February, 1906) they were ready to close their cargo hold and despite adverse weather forecasts they made arrangements to sail on Saturday morning's tide. For Robert Thomas, the Captain, this was a regular trip but at this time of year (in February) the weather could be at its worst. Robert was apprehensive of the weather when around breakfast time on Saturday morning they were towed by a steam-tug through the lock-pits into the River Mersey. As they headed North-Westward under tow towards Liverpool Bar light-vessel the wind was blowing steadily from the South West at what appeared to be a moderate working breeze. The skies were overcast and Captain Thomas considered the options for his passage South. He knew that with the South Westerly wind direction he would have difficulty getting around the North Western corner of Anglesey and wanting to keep well clear of the notorious Skerries, near Holyhead, he took an early decision to head North West towards the Irish coast passing South of, and clearing, the Southern tip of the Isle of Man. From there he planned to turn South and keep close to the Irish Coast for the run South towards Lands End.

Around noon on Saturday they slipped the tow from the tug at the mouth of the River Mersey but as the day went on the moderate wind veered Westerly and decreased in strength. *Old Hunter* only made slow progress and before nightfall Captain Thomas knew that it was going to take some time to get to the Irish coast. The wind increased again to blow at moderate strength and backed into the South West for the remainder of the day, making their first night at sea comfortable enough, with only slight seas. It had been a cold night and as dawn broke on Sunday morning the sky appeared a sullen grey, with the wind still blowing from the South West. During that day little progress was made South towards their destination and Robert realised that with the adverse wind direction he was unlikely to clear the Calf of Man at the southern tip of the Isle of Man.

Reviewing the options Robert decided he would continue towards the eastern side of the island, keeping about 10 miles from the land. If the wind continued from the unfavourable South Westerly direction he may have to go North around the Point of Ayr at the northern tip of the island. Throughout Sunday it rained and with the visibility only around 3 miles just occasionally they glimpsed the East coast of the island, noting landmarks as visibility improved. As watches changed the weather continued with steady rain and South Westerly force 3 winds. The daylight was rapidly fading around 3.30 p.m. on that Sunday afternoon and rather than drift further with the contrary tidal stream pushing their vessel northwards away from their intended direction Robert called the crew on deck, having decided to anchor for the night. From their last visual sighting they knew they were North of the town of Douglas and had seen Clay Head in the distance so they eased the sheets and altered course, heading in towards the coast for an hour or so towards Laxey Bay. Around 7.00 p.m. and with the shore lights of Laxey just visible they took a depth sounding that showed they were in ten fathoms of water. With all four crew again on deck the anchor was prepared. Sails were adjusted on *Old Hunter* to slow her down and bring her up into the wind and when they were ready the anchor was released. The anchor held on the sea-bed and having checked they were firmly anchored an anchor light was lit, hoisted up the mast and everyone settled into the anchor watch-keeping routine.

Before midnight the rain had stopped and the moon emerged fleetingly through the clouds. Visibility improved and the lights along the shoreline could be seen twinkling clearly in the distance. The night was uneventful and at daybreak around 8.00 a.m. on Monday morning Robert again considered their situation. He felt there was no need to hurry as the tidal stream would change in their favour within the hour, so he decided to remain at anchor and get the crew working on a number of deck jobs before they recovered the anchor around 10.00 a.m. The intention was then to set sail and head south east away from the Manx coast. The morning proved to be an unpromising day with grey leaden skies and the wind stubbornly remained in the South West. With gaff fore and main sails set, along with the fore topsail and jibs, *Old Hunter* was sailing as well as they could expect but not in their intended direction, going further eastward than they hoped to be. As the day went on they saw a change in the sky as dark clouds appeared behind them on the Western horizon. By 3.00 p.m. they could see the outline of the Cumbrian coast on their port side. This was home ground for Robert, who hailed from Barrow-in-Furness, so he felt familiar with the contours of this coastline. Although the weather was looking increasingly unsettled the wind had started to veer more westerly. He wasn't concerned because he could just reduce sail and spend the night between the Manx coast and the Western shores of Cumbria that he had grown up with. Black Combe was visible on their port side at a range of around 20 miles. Anticipating a change for the worse in the weather he tried to get a couple of hours sleep in his cabin as he expected he might have to be available on deck for much of the night. Fresh supplies had been taken on board in Liverpool and they were looking forward to a hot meal that evening. At 6.00 p.m. and before they sat down for their evening meal Robert decided to get the crew on deck to shorten sail for the night; reefing the gaff main and foresails, shortening the square topsail and removing the jibs, just leaving a fore staysail set. It took some time to reduce the sails and frustratingly the wind had gone light by the time this task was completed. Robert had a lingering concern at the back of his mind that the dark clouds he had seen earlier to the West were signs of an adverse change in the weather. It was a dark night and no moon was visible. All four crew on board had worked to lower the sails and once completed with just John Hughes, the Mate, standing watch on deck the other three on board went down into the saloon and started their meal that had been keeping warm in the galley oven. Within the hour and before he was due to be relieved on watch by Robert he called down through the skylight that the wind was freshening from the West. Less than half an hour later when Robert came on deck to take the watch the wind was Westerly force 6. Although he decided not to put more sail on he did decide to alter course to head further South and get some advantage from the wind shift. All hands were again called on deck to assist with adjusting the sail sheets to settle *Old Hunter* down on their new course. With all changes completed crewman Charles Hakeman was left on lookout with Robert and the other two settled down in their bunks to get some sleep before they were called for their watch at midnight. Less than an hour later the wind started gusting ferociously and veering into the North West, each gust becoming stronger and approaching gale force. The seas began to increase and an uncomfortable rolling motion began. On board *Old Hunter* a sense of foreboding was developing amongst the four crew members. Although heading South and with plenty of sea-room the wind seemed to be strengthening at an alarming rate. It then started to rain and this became heavier and heavier, at times with sleet and hail mixed in. The sudden deterioration of the weather gave Robert a sense that worse was to follow and desperate to avoid the lee shore of the Duddon Sands he felt that the North Westerly wind would favour them in heading South. Around 10.30 p.m. the crew were again called on deck to effect another course change, with the need to adjust the sheets once more. Even though they had sou-westers, oilskin smocks and boots on, the driving rain seemed to seep into their clothing until they were wet to their skin.

Across the darkness of that night and not 10 miles away another aging collier, the *Maggie Kelso* was facing the same change in weather. They had sailed on Monday morning, also from Liverpool and along with other vessels the schooner *Maggie Kelso*, having cleared the River Mersey, was heading Northwards for Dalbeattie in Scotland on the North coast of the Solway Firth. She was owned by Messrs. George Wilson and Sons of Dalbeattie and this was her home port. The South Westerly breeze had been favourable for their passage but she was only sluggish as she was in need of a new suit of sails and ready for her bottom scraping of the seaweed growth that had accumulated on the hull below the waterline over more than a year. John Taylor the captain of the 58 ton schooner *Maggie Kelso* was having the same misgivings over the change in the weather as the wind shift into the West was making things more difficult for him as they tried to progress

Northwards. When he came on deck to take over the watch at 8.00 p.m. he was considering anchoring for the night but the gusting wind seemed to be a portend of imminent worsening weather. The next half hour saw a dramatic increase in the wind strength and the direction veered into the North West. John Taylor sensed they were in for a bad night and wanted to be decisive and prudent in his actions. As they were roughly North West of the entrance to Morecambe Bay he considered his options and chose to head East to take shelter and anchor in the Bay to ride out the storm and wait for an improvement in the weather.

On board *Old Hunter* their sense of foreboding increased when a violent gust of wind hit them, pushing them off course and broadside to the wind, causing their vessel to heel over alarmingly to port. The gust of wind passed and *Old Hunter* slowly rolled back upright again. The helmsman struggled to bring her back on course but as Robert was helping tighten in the sheets that had been freed he had in his mind a feeling that things were likely to get worse before they got better. Within minutes another squall hit them and again *Old Hunter* veered off course and heeled over as violently as before. This confirmed in Robert's mind that he needed to anticipate more of these gusts and continue to head Eastwards towards Morecambe Bay to gain some shelter. This hadn't been an easy thing for them to do. He had been reluctant to gybe *(a method of sail adjustment to change the vessels direction)* their vessel with the risk of another squall hitting them while they were doing this and so with all crew again called on deck they had turned *Old Hunter* into the wind to go about through the wind and head east on a new course. In Robert's mind he was intending to further reduce sail on this new course but soon after they had come about another squall struck and they surged along before the wind at an alarming rate. The wind had now reached gale force and although Robert thought it was a squall that would soon pass the wind continued to steadily increase and he was concerned that they would have difficulty shortening sail. He decided to stand on and run before the wind with the existing sails set, hoping to see the navigation lights of Morecambe Bay. The wind continued to blow at gale force and with driving hail but with the wind further aft and behind them it hadn't seemed as bad on their backs. At one point they reassuringly caught sight of Walney Light and knowing the area he had expected that they would soon see the light of Gassoon (now Lightning Knoll) buoy. By now the seas were rising and crested waves were breaking around them but with the wind astern they continued to make good speed. Around midnight the loom of Lune Light vessel was seen ahead and they altered course to keep it on their starboard bow. Soon after seeing the light vessel a violent hail storm hit them and visibility was reduced to almost zero but within twenty minutes the hail had ceased and once again they had reasonable visibility against a dark sky that no moon was able to penetrate. Passing Lune Light vessel on their starboard beam around 00.30 a.m. they turned East North East to head towards Wyre Light. The wind had increased to severe gale force 9 and rain was again reducing visibility so it was impossible to see any features on the coast. Running before the wind and seas for half an hour without any sighting of Wyre Light Robert called all crew on deck as he was becoming concerned they would need to alter course, reduce sail, and prepare to anchor on the edge of Lune Deep. For a moment the rain stopped, with the sky clearing sufficiently for them to see a flash of Wyre Light but not in the place they had expected to see it. Robert shouted orders to the helmsman to turn to port and as soon as *Old Hunter* came broadside to the seas they appreciated the violence of the weather and the height of the breaking seas. An order was shouted to Charles to take a depth sounding with the lead-line. Within minutes Charles hurried back to report that there was only 30 feet of water beneath them. Robert realised they were making excessive leeway and had been driven south of Lune Deep onto the banks of Shell Wharf. Suddenly their situation was becoming desperate as they tried to steer North East to regain the deep water channel but the strength of the wind was causing further leeway and they were being pushed sideways towards the sandbanks. The waves were becoming breaking surf as they tried to claw themselves northwards into deeper water but the fore topsail was being backed and the gaff fore and main were beginning to flap and lose the wind. Starting with the foretopsail the crew tried to adjust it to get it to fill but to no avail. In this extreme weather any change was difficult and despite their extreme efforts they were unable to regain control of the situation. Robert took over the helm himself so the helmsman could go and assist on deck but he was now realising the gravity of their situation. Over the howling wind they could hear the crash of waves breaking on the shore and suddenly it seemed only a matter of time before they would be amongst the white maelstrom of breaking surf. The impact happened sooner than anyone had expected and there was a deafening sound as the keel struck the seabed. The suddenness of this grounding knocked everyone off their feet, apart from Robert who was braced against the wheel. The other three crew on board found themselves in the scuppers against the starboard rail, entangled in the ropes and sheets and struggling to regain their feet. Robert himself had also lost his footing but clung to the wheel with both hands, as with *Old Hunter* heeled dramatically to starboard he tried to get back his control at the wheel. The hull continued to move as every wave crashed against its sides. The sound of the sails flapping and beating in this *'flaying machine'* of wind was tremendous and within minutes the gaff main sail was rent horizontally with large pieces of canvas flapping uncontrollably in the wind that made the masts *'buckle and leap'*. Everyone on board was fearful for their lives as the keel was pounded repeatedly on the seabed by the waves that were breaking right across *Old Hunter's* decks. With the crashing sound of their ship striking the hard sandbank the hull shuddered and trembled *'like a house of cards about to collapse at any moment'*. Robert called all hands aft to set off distress rockets to summon assistance and prepare themselves for what could be the imminent destruction of their ship. It was difficult to get the rocket into its launcher but with great skill they eventually ignited the fuse that suddenly fired the rocket into the night sky. The blue light bursting above them revealed a chaotic scene with sails flying uncontrollably, spume blowing from the wave crests and the line of surf that lay between them and the shoreline. Another rocket was rapidly sent up and having done all they could the mate and two crew-members lashed themselves to the base of the main mast. Before joining the others at the mast Robert lit a storm lantern and hoisted it up the main mast as a signal. For what seemed to be an eternity nothing appeared to happen, yet the wind blew unforgivingly across the decks and the waves bounced and lifted the hull, inching it further onto the sandbank with thunderous sounds as each wave dropped the hull heavily again onto the seabed. The strain on the wooden hull was tremendous and a loud crash was heard above the wind and waves as some of the main beams broke as the hull was squeezed by the forces of the extreme weather. All four on board had started to shiver uncontrollably due to a combination of shock, being soaked to their skin and fear for their lives. Suddenly, from an easterly direction on the shore John, the mate saw a green star rocket momentarily in the sky over the shore and shouted to the others that their distress rockets had been seen. Around the same time, and somewhat insidiously, the crashing sounds from the hull diminished and within minutes they realised that the hull was gripped on the sandbank and the bouncing had ceased as the tide was receding. The noise was still terrific as the wind howled in the rigging and the sails flapped noisily with whip-cracking sounds but the motion had stopped and Robert released himself from the lashing that had bound him to the mast. He crawled across the deck to the ships side and although it was pitch dark he could see the white tops of the waves but he noticed that although they were still breaking across the decks on the for'ard part of the ship it was less so down at the aft end. Creeping back across the deck a feeling of calm welled up inside him as for the first time in that awful hour he felt that the hull of *Old Hunter* could survive and that rescue may be possibly at hand. He stretched his arms around the base of the mast as he shouted above the wind to tell the crew his findings that the hull was firmly embedded on Shell Wharf bank and the tide was ebbing away from their vessel.

On board the schooner *Maggie Kelso*, John Taylor the master and the two crew members were surprised at how quickly the weather deteriorated as before 9 o' clock that evening the wind had increased to full gale force from the North West. Having abandoned their intentions of pushing North every minute of the worsening weather confirmed to John that he was doing the right thing by heading for shelter in Morecambe Bay. His plan was to head for shelter under Piel Island off the north coast of Morecambe Bay. They had just settled onto their new course, reduced and trimmed their sails and walked aft when a sudden squall caught them with such violence that with an enormous bang the main boom broke under the pressure of wind, causing the main sail to collapse uselessly without the support of the boom. John Taylor immediately sent Bill and Andrew to the mast to lower the now useless mainsail while he took the wheel and brought their vessel up into the wind. From the steering position John shouted orders above the rising storm to drop the main that was flapping and flagging out of control. The boom had broken roughly halfway along its length and nothing could be done in the atrocious conditions to make any temporary repair. He wasn't familiar with this part of the coast and without the assistance of the mainsail he realised he would be unable to continue in the direction of Piel, so he turned Southeast and down-wind to head towards Lune Deep and the entrance to Morecambe Bay, where he hoped to anchor while the storm abated. He had studied his chart and committed to memory the distinctive difference in the pattern of lights. Previously he expected to see the beam from Walney Light looming from the darkness but he now had to consult the chart again for this new approach. The visibility was poor for them and in the hail storms that were frequently reducing their visibility to less than 50 yards they were struggling to see where they were. As the night went on and shortly after midnight, the first light pattern they caught sight of was believed to be the Lune Light vessel. They expected to see it ahead of them and the fact that it was well on their port bow indicated to them that they were being pushed too far South. No sooner had they sighted the light than another hail squall closed in the visibility but within minutes and while John was considering their situation the visibility cleared to reveal the light that they confirmed to be Lune Light vessel and rapidly realised the difficulty they were in. All three of those on board were standing together clustered around the steering position and John ordered Bill to take the wheel and alter course to North East while he and Andrew adjusted the sheets to tighten the fore sail. Without the benefit and drive from the mainsail on this new course whilst trying to sail closer to the wind the waves were crashing over the port bow and everything seemed so much worse than it had been for the past three hours. Without the mainsail the seas crashing on the bow were stopping the forward movement of *Maggie Kelso* and she started to make excessive leeway, crabbing sideways, towards the shore. Their fate now seemed inevitable and the events taking place appeared to be happening in slow motion until with a thundering crash and rending grind the hull struck the seabed and bounced with alarming noise; the impact causing a shudder to resonate throughout the hull. They considered launching their rowing boat but instinct told them to set off a distress rocket to alert those on shore to their dilemma. As the rocket burst above them, momentarily illuminating the scene with dramatic effect, the wind rapidly carried the illumination away from them. This left them once again in inky darkness, not knowing exactly where they were and doubtful if anyone had seen their distress signal in the poor visibility as the hail continued to drive unrelentingly at them.

From the shore on Fleetwood Promenade the blue lights had been seen and understood to be distress signals. The observer ran to the Coastguard houses to summon assistance and the coastguards dressed and ran to the seafront with a telescope. As they arrived on the Promenade they saw a distress rocket but not from the direction originally reported by the fisherman who had stayed with them and was present beside them on the seafront. The chief coastguard sent a runner with a message to Coxswain David Leadbetter, who was in charge of the lifeboat *Maude Pickup.* Coxswain Leadbetter received the message shortly before 2 o'clock early on Tuesday morning that at least one and possibly two vessels were showing signals of distress in Morecambe Bay. Leadbetter immediately rushed to the lifeboat station and fired the explosive signals to assemble a crew. Within a short time men came running to the lifeboat-house from different directions and in a very few minutes the places available in the lifeboat were filled up. Coxswain Leadbetter stated "we could have had five crews without difficulty". At 2.15 a.m. the *Maude Pickup* had been launched and was proceeding towards the distressed vessels in tow of the steam tug *Fylde*, belonging to the Joint Railway Companies. The wind was blowing from North-North-West, and there was a nasty sea and some heavy squalls and hail showers.

At an agreed signal the tug slipped it's towline to the lifeboat midway between the Wyre Light and King Scar buoy. The lifeboat then set sail and bore down to the schooner that had been reported to be somewhere in the direction of Shell Wharf. As they cleared King Scar buoy the bowman noticed a pinpoint of light and he called to David Leadbetter, pointing with his arm outstretched to indicate something on the lifeboat's port bow that proved to be a faint light. The lifeboat altered course and proceeded South-South-West to investigate. The tide was ebbing and the coxswain was concerned about how much water they had beneath them and edged Westward to ensure sufficient sea-room. The wind at this time was severe gale force, coming from the North West by West. Spume was being torn from the wave crests in eddying swirling patches, making visibility difficult for the lifeboat as they tried to keep the weak light in view ahead of them.

A heavy sea was running around Rossall Point with breaking surf on the sandy shore and the hull of *Old Hunter* had been pounding on the seabed. She was ashore on some boulders, off Shell Wharf. When the lifeboat arrived the breaking waves showed them it was too shallow to get near the schooner's hull in the surf. They could make out the name that proved to be the *Old Hunter*. Coxswain Leadbetter decided to wait for more water and 'stand by' for an hour. They lowered their sails, raised the keel and using the oars prepared to let go of their anchor.

Schooner *Old Hunter*

Within half an hour as the tide came slowly in they took soundings and decided to approach the *Old Hunter* - the time being 3.30 a.m. - and they got alongside the *Old Hunter* on the starboard side. The continuous surf and the shallow water made the rescue very difficult, but they managed to get the crew of four on board the lifeboat. At the time of launching they were aware of the possibility of another incident nearby and by chance saw another light further South. When they left *Old Hunter* they made towards it to investigate further and found there to be another other schooner in distress, which was about a mile away, beyond Rossall Point. She proved to be *Maggie Kelso* and they found the vessel in about 5 feet of water. As the Maud Pickup life-boat required about 12 feet to move about in safety, they could not reach her at this time. They could see men on the stern but as the hull was close into the shore they knew those on-board were not in imminent danger.

Coxswain Leadbetter thought that it would be best to land the four sailors from the *Old Hunter* at Fleetwood, and by the time they could return there would be sufficient water to get to the other vessel. Coxswain Leadbetter stated "we accordingly signalled the tug and she took us in tow. We landed the men on the beach near the lifeboat house at 5.20 a.m." Looking at his exhausted crew as they we shuffling out of their lifebelts he knew he must put it to them that they had to return to the *Maggie Kelso.* In a few blunt sentences he said to them that they could remain on-board the lifeboat for the return to the *Maggie Kelso*, or, without any recrimination be relieved and replaced by another man. The exhausted men saw the need, and, tired as they were, battered as some of them had been, they were prepared to face the howling gale again. Even as they nodded or growled their readiness they knew that conditions might get even worse than on the previous trip, for the tide was higher. However, they had already achieved the seemingly impossible that day under Coxswain David Leadbetter, and they were ready to face the elements again. Without leaving the boat the lifeboat-men, seeing human lives were at stake, struggled back into their wet oilskins and cork lifebelts, tied their cold sou'westers under their chins, and prepared for the grim battle all over again. They at once proceeded on their life-saving mission, taken in tow again by the steam-tug *Fylde.* According to Coxswain Leadbetter: "As we neared the vessel we again put our anchor out. We managed to get near the schooner on the port side. The three sailors were in a hurry to get off their vessel, as they jumped into the lifeboat really before the *Maude*

Pickup had got alongside the vessel. The broken seas again made the rescue very difficult and we were deluged with water". They arrived back in Fleetwood harbour at 7.20 a.m., landing the men at the Fleetwood ferry slip. At 8.15 a.m., for the third time they again left the harbour, in tow of the steam-tug *Lune*. This time they proceeded to the vessel *Maggie Kelso* in the hope of saving her. They put six men on board, and succeeded in getting lines attached. As the tide came in she floated, and was brought into Fleetwood.

Coxswain Leadbetter added that he had been a lifeboatman for 24 years and Coxswain for 11 years and in all his experience he had never had to rescue people under such difficult conditions in regard to broken sea and shallow water. The Fleetwood boat was one of the largest owned by the Institution and had a deep draft, therefore special care had to be taken in approaching the vessels. The lifeboat crew did their work well and 7 people were rescued without sustaining any injury. The skipper of the *Maggie Kelso* was warm in his praise of the conduct at the lifeboat crew.

Schooner *Old Hunter* aground along with Schooner *Maggie Kelso*

When the tide ebbed the *Old Hunter* stood high and dry on the sands about a mile away from the promenade. Many people visited the battered craft during the afternoon. She resting comfortably on the even sands and on inspection of the vessel showed that she had shipped a lot of water. Mr. Singleton, a boat builder, and his men were engaged on the schooner all afternoon and a good deal of water was pumped and drained from the vessel. As it approached the time of high water, the *Old Hunter* floated and she was brought into the harbour by a tug.

The names of the men who went out in the *Maude Pickup* were:- Messrs. D. Leadbetter (coxswain), R. Wright (bowman), W. Wright, E. Salthouse, R. Salthouse, T. Leadbetter, J. Leadbetter, R. Wright, J. Price, J. Roskell, J. Cross, T. Snape, J. Wright, J. Mason, and T. Preston.

The names of the rescued men were:- Robert Thomas, Captain of the *Old Hunter*; John Hughes, mate; Charles Hakeman and John Turner; John Taylor, captain of *Maggie Kelso*; A. Currie and W. Neilson. The men were taken to Mr. Johnston's restaurant, and afterwards to the Sailor's Rest, and were well looked after by Messrs. J.N. Ward and Sons, the local agents of the Shipwrecked Mariners Society.

The distress rockets had also been seen from Barrow and the Piel lifeboat reached the *Old Hunter* only to find the crew had been taken off.

Captain Jackson, the harbour master and marine superintendent was praised for promptly ordering the tug boats to turn out. The tugs greatly assisted the lifeboat in the rescue work.

When Coxswain David Leadbetter became ill in the Summer of 1906 second coxswain John Robert Leadbetter became acting coxswain. One of the last service calls David Leadbetter undertook was on 19th November 1906 when in hurricane force conditions the lifeboat *Maude Pickup* rescued the crew from the trawler *Belmont* (FD64) that had been driven onto Pilling Sands. The lifeboat had been launched two days earlier on 17th November to take off the crew when she grounded and was again launched when a crew had been put back on board by local boats to attempt to re-float the *Belmont* but the weather deteriorated and all those on board had to be rescued.

Lifeboat *Maude Pickup* rescue from Steam Trawler *Belmont*

John Robert Leadbetter coxswain 1909 - 1923

Lifeboat Coxswain John Robert Leadbetter

John Robert Leadbetter was appointed coxswain in 1909, having been acting coxswain for three years. He was one of seven brothers and had been second coxswain when his brother David was coxswain. He retired in 1923 having served 14 years as coxswain, having been on the crew for 41 years. He had been second coxswain of the *Maude Pickup* lifeboat during the rescue in June 1897 when 18 people were saved from the vessels *Svalen*, *Louise* and *Zillah*. Just like David Leadbetter during each summer for a number of years he was recruited to skipper a large yacht. She was the *Wallaroo* and was unbeaten under his command, in the Whitsuntide race to Ramsey, Isle of Man, which always started at midnight from Fleetwood. *Wallaroo's* owner, wealthy businessman Mr. Spurr said of him at John Robert's funeral 'I am proud to have met one of England's gentlemen'.

October 25th, 1917. Russian barque *'Pittan'*.

A notable rescue took place in October 1917 when the barque *Pittan* was wrecked on Pilling Sands. A terrific gale from the West-North-West swept over Fleetwood on Wednesday night 25th October and

Thursday morning, doing considerable damage to property in various parts of the town, causing damage to several hoardings.

Shortly before one o'clock, in the early hours of Thursday morning, signals of distress were observed from the direction on Lune Deep. In response the harbour tug, *Cleveleys* went out but failed to locate the whereabouts of the vessel. The *Cleveleys* continued the search until daybreak, when the crew observed the Russian barquentine, *Pittan.* This vessel left Fleetwood the previous Friday, loaded with a cargo of pitch for Spain. Due to adverse weather changes she had turned around and returned to Lune Deeps and was drifting onto Pilling Sands.

Maude Pickup rescue from Russian barque *Pittan* October 1917

Shortly before 7.00 a.m. the Fleetwood lifeboat *Maude Pickup* was launched to assist the apparently doomed vessel, which by that time had drifted on to the Sands, abreast of Fluke Hall and was quickly becoming a wreck. Despite the adverse weather and rough seas, Coxswain John Robert Leadbetter skillfully handled the lifeboat and in just over half an hour had reached the barquentine, which was full of water and breaking up.

The seven crew members including the skipper were on the poop. Six of the crew had been hauled into the lifeboat when the hawser to which the lifeboat was fastened to the barquentine broke. After several attempts the lifeboat crew succeeded in again coming alongside the vessel and despite considerable difficulty the captain was rescued.

The crew of the *'Pittan'* were brought back to Fleetwood in the lifeboat, and taken by Mr. M. J. Wedum, secretary of the Shipwrecked Mariners' Society, to Johnston's Dining Rooms, where they were provided with a substantial meal and dry clothing. They were in an exhausted condition and drenched to the skin. The men were taken charge of by Mr G. Simpson, the Port Missionary, who, acting on behalf of the British and Foreign Sailors' Society provided them with complete outfits.

The vessel had apparently broken its anchor cable at about midnight and despite the efforts of the crew drifted rapidly on to the Sands.

Shipwrecked Crew's thanks to Fleetwood Lifeboat and to the Townspeople for Universal Kindness

The master of the Russian vessel *'Pittan'*, wrecked on Pilling Sands during a storm of last week and the crew that were saved by the Fleetwood Lifeboat forwarded the following letter, expressing thanks to the Fleetwood lifeboat crew and to the people of Fleetwood for the way they had been treated. High tribute was paid to the behaviour of the lifeboat crew and to the way the boat was handled:-

Dear Sir, - I shall feel obliged if you will allow me through the medium of your paper to express the heartfelt gratitude of myself and my crew for the splendid work done by the Fleetwood lifeboat and her noble and brave crew, in recuing us from the dangerous position we were placed in when my vessel went ashore on Pilling Sands on Thursday morning 26th October.

The way in which the lifeboat was handled, under the difficulties in which the storm and the shallow water placed her, was something marvellous, and if she had not been handled as she was it would have been quite impossible for any of us to get on board, as we were too exhausted and frozen to be able to attempt to swim.

Our thanks are also due to the Shipwrecked Mariners' Society, whose representative cared for us immediately on landing and to the British and Foreign Sailors Society, who, through their representative, Mr. Simpson, furnished us with clothing and comforts.

I must also thank the people of Fleetwood for their universal kindness, and for the reception they gave us on landing from the lifeboat.

Yours respectfully,

Karl Behrsin

Master of the Russian Vessel, *'Pittan'*

Another letter had also been received by Mr. Simpson, the Fleetwood Representative of the British and Foreign Sailors' Society:-

Dear Sir, - We wish to express to you, and through you to the Society you represent, our very best and heartfelt thanks for the kindness you have shewn to us since we were landed hers by the lifeboat after our ship, the Russian vessel *'Pittan'*, had gone ashore on Pilling Sands, when you were good enough to furnish us with outfit of clothing, having nothing left but the soaked clothes in which we landed.

Yours respectfully,

Karl Behrsin, Master

Wilslip Pommer Mate

Tethan Krastan Coxswain

Wilen Ewert Sailor

Oswald Behrsin Sailor

Mikal Jansen Sailor

James Goldring, Cook

Fleetwood lifeboat crew, coxswain John Robert Leadbetter circa 1910

The above photograph was taken around the time that Coxswain John Robert Leadbetter took over from his brother David Leadbetter. The 1911 census shows that John Robert, along with his wife Ann and their seven children, were living at 9 Pharos Street, Fleetwood.

William Wright coxswain 1923 - 1933

Lifeboat Coxswain William Wright

William Wright was appointed coxswain in 1923 when John Robert Leadbetter retired. William served as coxswain for ten years and retired in 1933. He was part of the fishing family who had moved from Marshside, Southport to Fleetwood in the nineteenth century. He was coxswain of the *Maude Pickup* lifeboat when on Christmas night 1929 the lifeboat was called upon to rescue six people from the former liner *Tchad.* His son Richard Wright who became coxswain in the 1960's was a crew member for this service call.

Although William reached retirement age in 1933 he continued to help in the boathouse when the lifeboat was called out. During the Second World War he served as 'Launcher' but was injured while 'knocking out' the release shackle when the chain broke his arm. Following this accident he died from complications arising from this injury on 4th June, 1945.

The photograph over the page shows the lifeboat crew around 1925, with William as coxswain.

Fleetwood lifeboat crew with coxswain William Wright circa 1925

William Wright was coxswain of Fleetwood Lifeboat when the picture below was taken on Lifeboat Saturday July 1929. William is standing on the promenade outside the former lifeboathouse. The picture shows a young girl Grace Crossthwaite with a collecting box and lifeboat pin-badges. On her left is lifeboat-house attendant Mr Harry 'Onward' Leadbetter. Throughout her adult life she was a dedicated supporter of the R.N.L.I, serving as Chair of the Fleetwood branch of the Ladies Lifeboat Guild. Her husband Bert Crossthwaite was Winchman for many years. Son Victor was a volunteer crew member and became a full-time Relief Mechanic and eventually joined the Coastguard Service.

Lifeboat Saturday July 1929

Wednesday December 25th, 1929. Drifting French Liner *Tchad*

The lifeboat service is always available 365 days a year. In this incident Fleetwood Lifeboatmen effected a brave and gallant rescue on Christmas night, 1929. In the teeth of a south-westerly gale the lifeboat, manned by a crew of fifteen, was launched in response to distress signals from Lune Deeps. It had been seven years since the Fleetwood lifeboat *Maude Pickup* had been called out on a rescue incident and the lifeboat was reported to have performed extremely well. Apart from routine exercises the last rescue call out the *Maude Pickup* had been launched was on December 6th, 1922.

French Liner *Tchad*

The French liner Steam Ship *Tchad* of Le-Havre was a vessel of about 6,000 tons register. Purchased by Messrs. Ward, of Preston and Morecambe, she had been towed from Bordeaux by the Hull tug *"Seaman,"* on her way to be broken up for scrap at Morecambe. They arrived on Saturday afternoon 21st December in Lune Deeps, where she was moored about two miles to the north of Wyre Light. When during Christmas Day the weather deteriorated the liner began to drag her anchor and she slowly drifted across Morecambe Bay in the direction of Grange-over-Sands. At around 5.00 p.m. the gale increased in violence and the ship's master Captain Thomas Neilson Murray, who was on board with five others, ordered all the crew on deck. James Jackson, an engineering fitter from Morecambe who joined the steamer on Sunday 22nd of December, was working below with John Atkinson, also a fitter from Morecambe. They knew nothing of what was happening on deck until the skipper shouted down the speaking tube: 'Come up at once and save yourselves. The ship is drifting.' They both dropped the tools they were working with and ran on deck dressed just as they were, almost stripped to the waist. They saw that the steamer was drifting in the gale, which blew so hard that they could scarcely hear each other speak.

The Captain and another crew member had already paid out 150 fathoms of chain in the hope that the anchor would hold again, but it did prevent the ship from drifting. The vessel began to list heavily to port and it looked as if she might capsize. Distress rockets were then fired but did not appear to attract any answer from the shore. Those on board could just see the shorelights of Fleetwood. Realising things were getting serious, they brought up the mattresses from the beds, placed them on the ship's lifeboat, soaked them in paraffin and set them alight. As fast as one mattress burnt itself out they threw on another, burning six altogether. The ship's lifeboat, which was a steam engined one, also got partly alight as the flames spread. They all sheltered behind some deck casing, straining their eyes to see if they had been seen. It was a tremendous relief when they saw signal rockets go up from the lifeboat-house at Fleetwood, indicating in response that their distress had been seen. As the weather became worse Captain Murray, who was on the bridge, ordered the men below decks.

Even in the atrocious weather of that day the distress rockets from the *Tchad* had been seen by the light-keepers on Wyre Light. Shortly after 5.00 p.m. on Christmas Day flares were sent up from the Lighthouse, about two miles out at sea, as the keepers had observed the plight of the big steamer and were signaling to attract attention from the shore. The distress signals from the *Tchad* and the flares from Wyre Light had also been observed by Henry Girvin, who lived at 11, Macbeth Road Fleetwood, when he was walking along the Fleetwood Promenade on the lookout for a trawler whose return from the fishing grounds was expected. He ran to the Coastguard houses near the Mount, to inform them of the incident and returned to the Promenade with the coastguard officers to report the direction he had seen the distress signals from.

The lifeboat rocket was fired, and within a few minutes a large number of men had rushed to the lifeboat to volunteer their services. One youthful member of the crew who had left a family Christmas party and gone out in his 'Sunday best,' in order to arrive early at the lifeboat-house. To make sure of a life-jacket and place on the boat he had dashed straight from the family gathering at home on a push-bike. His relatives shouted that they would follow him down to the lifeboat-house as quickly as they could with warmer clothes but they hadn't arrived with the rest of his clothes when the lifeboat was launched. Without the protection of oilskin 'slickers,' his suit was practically ruined by the time they returned.

Coxswain William Wright explained that a mishap occurred when the boat was launched that might have cost the lives of two or three lifeboat-men. When the *Maude Pickup* left the slipway the crew were in the act of raising and securing the mizzen mast when a bolt came out of its socket, causing the mast to come crashing down. Fortunately it did not strike any of the crewmen in its fall, otherwise there might have been fatal injuries. As they rowed down the river the crew were barely conscious of the stinging hail, as the icy spray whipped up by the gale was flung continuously over the open lifeboat. Each crew member pulled and pushed the heavy oars, jarred by each blow of the sea and thrown about by the steep pitching of the lifeboat. Snow and sleet was driven relentlessly at them by the gale force winds. Their ears, fingers and toes were numbed by the cold. Water had filled the crew-mens' boots but the boat's motion was so violent they couldn't empty them. At one moment they were climbing a great wall of water at an angle that threatened to shoot every man forwards into the sea; the next, the boat had tipped into the trough of the seas, almost standing on her bows. Through mountainous seas the lifeboat ploughed its way to the aid of the disused large liner.

Before they reached the top of the channel they lowered the drop-keel, turned the lifeboat into wind and hoisted their sails. With all sails set they hauled on the sheets and resumed course down channel towards Lune Deep. They sailed across the Bay until they approached the steamer, which they found lying in Lune Deeps with one anchor out near to No. 1 buoy at the entrance to Heysham channel.

Lifeboat *Maude Pickup* approaching Liner *Tchad* painting by Ken Frost

For those on board the *Tchad*, though it was only 8.30 p.m. it was becoming a terrifying night. It had seemed hours before those on board saw what proved to be the lifeboat sailing towards them, bobbing up and down in the rough sea.

Progress was slow due to the atrocious weather conditions but at around 9.00 p.m., after more than two hours of back-and spirit breaking effort, they had reached the *Tchad*. As the lifeboat came close to the liner the coxswain sailed under the stern, pulling up to assess the situation, whilst bringing the lifeboat round to the lee side to gain shelter behind the hull of the *Tchad*.

At first those on board the *Tchad* saw the lifeboat sailing past them and they shouted as hard as they could to attract attention. When the lifeboat was close alongside the towering hull the coxswain hailed the captain and asked what he wanted. "He replied that they wished to get ashore." Coxswain Wright then manoeuvred the lifeboat as near as he could take the boat in safely, as tremendous seas were running, tossing the lifeboat up and down as though it were a cork. The lifeboat crew were kept busy putting out cork fenders along the port side, to prevent the boat from being violently dashed against the side of the ship that loomed above them out of the water like the walls of a tall building.

Lifeboat alongside Liner *Tchad*
painting Ken Frost

With the sails lowered the lifeboat's oars were used to bring the lifeboat alongside the hull of the steamer. A rope end was thrown down from the *Tchad* to the lifeboat but this broke and several minutes elapsed before another was procured and they were able to secure it. Four of the men from the steamer quickly lowered themselves by ropes into the lifeboat. The lifeboat could have been away very quickly, but the skipper and the sixth man were some time before they left the vessel. The coxswain then ordered the rope to be released and the lifeboat sheered off. Sails were hoisted and they set a course for home. The tide was ebbing fast and the lifeboat had to make a number of tacks before they got into the Wyre Channel. When they left the steamer *Tchad* it had a severe list to port, still with 150 fathoms of anchor chain paid out.

Although they we were out for over four hours the journey back to Fleetwood was far less strenuous, with the roaring gale behind them. As they entered the Fleetwood channel they had to stream and set the canvas drogue 'streamed' out behind them to steady the lifeboat in the breaking seas. The *Maude Pickup* lifeboat received a severe pounding, and not one of the occupants had a dry stitch of clothing on their backs. Despite their oilskins, most of the men were drenched to the skin from head to foot and their bodies numbed by the intense cold when they returned from their perilous mission.

Although it was Christmas Night a crowd had gathered on the Fleetwood Promenade, eagerly scanning the darkness for signs of the lifeboat. Soon after 9.00 p.m. they were rewarded by seeing white and green flares fired by Signalman George Mather from the lifeboat. The signal denoted that the lifeboat had reached her objective and was returning. As a long time elapsed and no further signals were received from the lifeboat, the harbour tug "Cleveleys" was commissioned to investigate. With steam already raised she left the pier-head shortly afterwards to search the Wyre Channel for news of the lifeboat and its crew. Before the tug was halfway down the channel they saw the lifeboat in the distance towards Wyre Light. The tug turned around and on her return she reported having seen the lifeboat and that she was returning. After six anxious hours of waiting the lifeboat came into sight, sailing up the Wyre channel and an hour later they had the *Tchad's* crew landed at Fleetwood.

The relief of the rescued at getting ashore was almost equalled by the relief the rescuers felt to be safely back after their gruelling contest with the elements. With their oilskin smocks flapping in the gale, they clasped the hands of their friends as they arrived on the shore. As rescuers and rescued came ashore from the lower landing stage near the landing stage at the North End Quay, which was home to Irish and Isle of Man passenger steamers and, later, the Pandoro and Stena ferries, another crowd awaited them and gave them hearty cheers and congratulations. The six rescued men were in a state of completed exhaustion and one had to be carried to the waiting taxi cab. Three of them were taken to their homes and the remaining three were given food and shelter at the Royal National Mission to Deep Sea Fishermen.

The lifeboat crew then made their way through the excited crowd to the boat-house, to shed their wet clothes. Having done this Dick 'Cush' Wright, soaked to the neck by the ordeal, gathered the crew to prepare to re-house the lifeboat. The crew were in an exhausted state but it had been a good Christmas Day's work. The boat was re-housed and ready for service. It was over and they could warm themselves up again to bring back feeling into their numb bodies and get something to eat and drink. Mr. Cartman, the Honorary Secretary, took the crew to his home where there was a bathroom and each of the crew took turns to immerse themselves in the warm water to restore the feelings to their bodies.

It was a happy ending to a remarkable Christmas night. Their strenuous effort had its reward, for six men had been taken into the *Maude Pickup* lifeboat. The stricken ship had been left at the mercy of the sea to contemptuously toss it on the beach the next day. However, when Boxing Day dawned the *Tchad* was visible on the skyline when looking across the bay from Fleetwood's Promenade. Apparently about seven miles out, she had drifted three or four miles from her moorings near Wyre Light towards Grange-over-Sands.

The lifeboat crew, who responded promptly to the call and effected the rescue, consisted of the following:-

Coxswain W. Wright, Fred Jackson, Ned Salthouse, Charles Price, R. W. Salthouse; T. Thomason, R. Wright, jnr., A. Wright, H. Leadbetter, J. Mathers, W. Sharp, W. ('Toby') Wright, L. Bond and M. Sumner.

The rescued men were:-

Thomas Neilson Murray, 10, Adelaide Street, Brentford, Middlesex, Master.

John Atkinson, 37, Cheapside, Morecambe, Electrician.

James Jackson, 1, South Bank, Morecambe, Fitter.

Christopher Stephenson, 3, Preston Street, Fleetwood.

Alfred Taylor, Blakiston Street West, Fleetwood, Seaman.

Harold MacDonald, Dock Chambers, 166, Dock Street, Fleetwood, Fireman.

Note: Inshore fisherman Richard Wright (who became coxswain in the 1960's) was a lifeboat crew member on the *S.S. Tchad* service and recalled that the wind was so strong that it snapped the tapes tying his sou-wester helmet, just after the lifeboat was launched. For hours at sea he had no head protection from the icy spray that lashed the lifeboat in the strong wind. Since that day he remained deaf in his left ear – the side exposed to the weather on that night.

Record of Service Rendered by lifeboat *Maude Pickup (1894-1930)*

December 22nd, 1894. Schooner *Annie Park* of Barrow. The three masted schooner apparently ran aground and was disabled with its sails blown away. Tug towed her into port.

December 22nd, 1894. Barque *Furu* on Pilling Sands This Norwegian barque *Furu* was built in 1873. She was registered in Norway at 844 tons and had a crew of fourteen. She was left high and dry after braving a hurricane in which she lost her topsail, forestay and mizzen stay sail, until 5.00 a.m., when the crew walked ashore. Her back was broken and keel torn away. She became a total wreck, sold later as salvage to local men. Captain Larsen made his report to the Receiver of Wrecks the next day.

June 16th, 1897. Barque *Svalen* of Tvedestrand. Aground on Sunderland Bank. Lifeboat towed by tug *Brock*.

Only 3 persons on board. All others had gone ashore previous day before storm blew up. Rescued three.

June 16th, 1897. After *Svalen* (above) went to barque *Louisa* of Drammen, aground on Pilling Sands. As the vessel was breaking up in pounding seas the lifeboat rescued crew of 9 plus Pilot.

June 16th, 1897. After *Svalen* and *Louisa* – spotted steamer *Zillah* of Liverpool also aground on Pilling Sands and appeared to be sinking rapidly. As lifeboat reached her she had already sunk. Two crew clinging to foremast. Other three hanging on to top of funnel.

All saved from incidents above and lifeboat landed 18 persons from the 3 incidents.

In recognition of the above incidents Coxswain David Leadbetter was awarded a pair of binoculars. Special bronze medals, given by a Birmingham gentleman, were later presented to each member of the gallant crew.

November 29th, 1897. Ship *Larnaca* of Nova Scotia. Distress signals near Pilling Sands. 90 mph winds.

(From 1897 to 1906 there was a 9 year gap when no rescue service launches were required.)

February 20th, 1906. *Old Hunter* of Barrow.

February 20th, 1906. *Maggie Kelso* of Dalbeattie.

November 17th, 1906. Trawler *Belmont.* Pilling Sands. Local boats went on. November 19th (2 days later) lifeboat rescued.

(No lifeboat rescue service were required from 1906 and into the First World War until 1917).

October 25th, 1917. Russian barque *Pittan.*

September 17th, 1920. Coaster *Waritar* of Chester. On fire.

December 6th, 1922. Trawler *Merrydale.*

December 25th, 1929. Steamship *Tchad.*

4 MOTOR LIFEBOATS *'SIR FITZROY CLAYTON'* (1933-1935) & *'FREDERICK H. PILLEY'* (1935-1939)

Fleetwood lifeboat station was temporarily closed from January 1930 to January 1933 while the slipway was rebuilt and the boathouse modified to take a motor-lifeboat, which was sent to the station on 15th January, 1933.

Fleetwood's first Motor Lifeboat *Sir Fitzroy Clayton*

The lifeboat *Sir Fitzroy Clayton* was stationed at Fleetwood from 15th January, 1933 to August 1935. As the first motor-lifeboat at the station she was 38 foot long and 9 foot 9 inches beam. Powered by a 35 horse power Tylor petrol engine that gave her a service speed of 7 knots. A service of inauguration was held on 1st July, 1933.

Syd Hill was appointed as mechanic.

The *Sir Fitzroy Clayton* lifeboat only served two and a half years at the Fleetwood station, during which time there were four service call-outs and 4 lives were saved.

The rescues undertaken by the lifeboats *Sir Fitzroy Clayton* and subsequently *Frederick H. Pilley* during their period of service at Fleetwood from 1933 to 1939 may of themselves appear unremarkable in the spectrum of incidents that have taken place in far more severe weather. Nonetheless for the individuals involved they were crucial lifesaving events for those people saved in each of the services rendered. They are included to give a perspective on the work of the lifeboat service.

Fleetwood lifeboat *Sir Fitzroy Clayton* was launched early on Sunday morning 20th May, 1934 to go to the help of the yacht *Wallaroo*, a competitor in the annual Whitsuntide race from Fleetwood to the Isle of Man organized by the Blackpool and Fleetwood Yacht Club.

Early in the yacht-race the *Wallaroo's* rigging failed causing the mainmast to fall down shortly after 6 a.m., when she was just 2 miles north of Lune buoy. Mr C.E. Tatham who was in charge of another yacht *Zulu*, that had departed from Fleetwood in the same race, lost sight of *Wallaroo* and turned round to investigate.

The race had started at 5.00 a.m. near Fleetwood Ferry slip and by 5.30 a.m. *Zulu* was around Wyre Light. Looking back they could see *Wallaroo* and another yacht that they could not distinguish. Around half an hour later they noticed something wrong with the *Wallaroo*. The wind was South Westerly force 4 to 5. At first they thought *Wallaroo's* crew were putting a reef in its mainsail but then they noticed her mast had disappeared altogether. Through their binoculars those on board *Zulu* saw that the mainmast and sail had gone and they immediately turned back to assist.

As they headed back towards *Wallaroo* they saw a distress rocket, confirming their fears that something was amiss. By the time they reached *Wallaroo* they saw that the bowsprit had broken off and Dr Redropp and his crew were recovering the mast, sail and rigging from the sea. Finding *Wallaroo* in a helpless condition the *Zulu* crew went to assist her, with the intention of towing her downwind towards Piel Island, Barrow. At the third attempt the *Zulu's* crew managed to pass a line to *Wallaroo* and commence a tow. With the wind direction it was decided to tow *Wallaroo* towards Piel Island.

The distress signals had been seen from the shore and Fleetwood Lifeboat was called out.

As the lifeboat launched down the slipway and entered the water; before she could get underway, the strong ebb tide caused her hull to strike the iron ladder on the perch at the foot of the slipway.

Lifeboat *Sir Fitzroy Clayton* slipway launch

The glancing blow made her list to starboard, tearing a whole approximately 2 feet long and 10 inches high near the port bow. She was holed above the waterline but continued with the rescue, staying out for four hours. Water immediately poured in, but this did not prevent coxswain Jeff Wright and his crew of seven from continuing to the assistance of the *Wallaroo.* Although her hull was waterlogged she remained buoyant despite serious damage just above the waterline. Coxswain Wright stated "We shipped heavy seas through the leak in the side almost continuously and our waterlogged condition retarded our progress. The water kept to one level. Eventually we sighted the *Zulu* with the *Wallaroo* in tow making for Piel, and we stood by them until they were safely berthed.

Fleetwood lifeboat came across yacht *Zulu* towing *Wallaroo* and accompanied them until they arrived and anchored in Piel Bight (Barrow), beneath the Castle ruins, at around 8.30 a.m. When the lifeboat went alongside *Zulu* the crew gave them 'cups of tea and cigarettes'.

Accompanying Mr C.E.Tatham on board *Zulu* were his son Mr Joseph Tatham, Mr T. Poynton, Mr Fred Burnett of Blackpool and Mr Edwin Rigby, a sailmaker, of Fleetwood.

15th September, 1934 Yacht *'Moonbeam'*

On Saturday evening 15th September, 1934 the lifeboat *Sir Fitzroy Clayton* rescued five people, including two women, from a small yacht *Moonbeam* aground near Wyre Light. The explosive report from the lifeboat maroons, summoning the lifeboat crew to assemble, brought a large crowd onto the promenade and beach beside the lifeboat station. Around the time that the lifeboat was launched the lightning flashes from a violent thunderstorm illuminated the scene enabling the lifeboat crew to catch glimpses of the yacht towards Wyre Light. The crowd's anxiety increased when, without warning, there was an electrical failure and the whole town was blacked out for a number of minutes.

The yacht *Moonbeam* had left Fleetwood earlier in the day on a pleasure cruise, with the intention of sailing to a point off the Blackpool coast where they would be able to get a spectacular view of the opening night switch-on of the Illuminations. About one mile from Wyre Light the yacht developed engine trouble and the owner Mr. Hilton put out his anchor but it failed to hold the seabed. He then went below to take off the engine cover to investigate. A few minutes later Mrs. Hilton went down into the cabin as Mr. Hilton had restarted the engine but on descending the stairs a coat on her arm caught in the engine's flywheel and she was dragged towards the engine. Mr. Hilton pulled her away and prevented any personal injury to his wife. For three hours those on board attempted to restart the engine but to no avail. As darkness fell the storm could be seen approaching the West and their drifting boat eventually grounded on a sandbank, where through being buffeted about she was in imminent danger of being broken to pieces by the heavy seas. Signals of distress were made and morse code signals were flashed by torch that were seen at Wyre Light. The lighthouse keepers communicated the situation to the officials on shore and the lifeboat was sent to the assistance of the stranded yacht. Mr. Hilton stated "the lifeboat arrived in the nick of time, for the weather was rapidly worsening, and our danger increased every minute."

The lifeboat *Sir Fitzroy Clayton* was launched for the last time on 28th August, 1935 and replaced by the new boat *Frederick H. Pilley.* After leaving Fleetwood Lifeboat Station the *Sir Fitzroy Clayton* lifeboat was anchored in the river, where she remained until the next day when she was taken by Coxswain Jeff Wright and his crew to Lytham to her new owner, Mrs. V. Thompson, of East Beach, who had her converted into a yacht.

Lifeboat *Sir Fitzroy Clayton*

Fleetwood Lifeboat Crew circa 1933

This crew photograph from 1933 shows coxswain Jeffrey Wright seated on a cannon located on the promenade beside the lifeboat-house. Standing (left to right) are Dick Abram, former coxswain William Wright, James Leadbetter, Richard Wright, Syd Hill and Barry Bond. Kneeling beside the cannon is Bill Houston. The lifeboat on station at this time was the *Sir Fitzroy Clayton.*

Record of Service Rendered by lifeboat *Sir Fitzroy Clayton* (1933-1935)

May 20th, 1934 Yacht *Wallaroo.*

September 15th, 1934. Motor boat *Moonbeam.*

October 7th, 1934. Motor Yacht *'535'* of Preston. Saved 4 lives.

May 29th, 1935. At sea for many hours in a vain search for a yacht reported to be missing.

Jeffrey Wright coxswain 1933 - 1948

David Pearce interviewed Jeffrey for a feature in the Fleetwood Chronicle in 1970 when he was a sprightly 83-year-old who recalled how he went down – as so many used to do – to see the lifeboat launched one February day in 1903.

Lifeboat Coxswain Jeffrey Wright

But that day he found himself with an oar in his hands – a 16-year-old volunteer on his first lifeboat shout. Under sail and oar the *Maude Pickup* travelled 26 miles that day in a full WSW storm to save all nine men from the barque *Vanadis* aground on the Sunderland Bank in heavy seas.

In 2016 David interviewed his son (also named Jeffrey) aged 92 who told him: "He was dedicated to the lifeboat cause all through his life. His interest was there until his death and dedicated is not too strong a word."

The family home was in Arthur Street close by the Pharos lighthouse and his son remembered: "He had a prawner called the *Mabel* and many a time I've seen him come home after 12 hours or more at sea wet through and dirty and he'd have a bath in the tin bath in front of the fire. My mother put a hot meal on the table but it would be interrupted by a policeman at the door wanting him to go in the lifeboat or sort out some maritime problem. He never refused."

Jeffrey has a fine painting by Fleetwood artist Robert Croft of the *Mabel* pictured near Steep Breast beach where the present day lifeboat station stands. But, unlike many Fleetwood schoolboys, he never went to sea with his Dad.

"My mother had been in domestic service as a young woman and perhaps it was this glimpse of what she saw then as a better life that made her determined I was not going to be a fisherman."

He passed the examination for Fleetwood Grammar School and a career in the Civil Service. His brother Frank was born in 1930.

" But as a young boy I went to the lifeboat house with Dad on Sundays and played on and around the lifeboat".

Jeffery Wright in latter years

"At the time he won his Silver Medal perhaps I didn't really appreciate what he had done. He was a quiet man who did not say much about his lifeboat work. But in my own later life I have looked back on his achievements with pride."

When David met Coxswain Wright nearly 50 years ago he also met his wife Mary who made him realise the stress families can face in waiting for the safe return of a lifeboat and her crew.

She explained: " When he came home I used to ask him – did you find the wreck? You left another one here at home!"

Like many fishermen, Jeffrey Wright could not swim.

He said: "You are more careful on a boat if you can't. I never once fell in but I fell on the deck one time and got one leg in!"

A favourite story concerned the time he was serving in the Royal Navy as mate onboard a minesweeping trawler in October, 1917. He had travelled home on leave through the night by train and arrived at five a.m. just as the maroons were fired to summon the lifeboat crew!

Jeffrey did not hesitate but dropped his kitbag and went to answer the call.

" Hello Jeffrey" said Coxswain John Robert Leadbetter, " where've you come from?"

"Lowestoft" was the terse reply. " By gum, you've been quick lad!"

The service was to the Russian barque *Pittan*, where seven sailors shinned down a rope over the stern of the stranded craft and jumped onboard the lifeboat.

Medals were awarded by the British and Foreign Sailors Society.

But there were no awards for a service which Jeffrey reckoned produced the worst ever conditions for him and his crew. It does not even appear on the honour boards which used to hang in the seafront lifeboat house.

One stormy night he and his crew went out to stand by a trawler called the *Sarba*.

" They recorded a wind speed on The Mount of 74 mph. A huge sea came and it swept right over us. When I got my breath back I realised I was still standing up at the wheel but only my head was above the water. There was no sign of anything or anybody else. Then a pair of heels floated up close to me. It was the mechanic floating more or less upside down and holding on to the engine room controls. I thought the other lads must have gone over the side but, amazingly, they had managed to hold on to something and they were all still onboard as we came up again on the swell and the water cleared off the lifeboat."

Jeffrey was 61 years old when he retired as Coxswain in 1948 but he was close on 70 when he last sailed in the lifeboat. He became a member of Station Committee and spent hours making toys from brightly coloured rope scraps which were sold in aid of R.N.L.I. funds.

This picture on page 99 was taken following the service with the *Ann*

Letitia Russell lifeboat to the Faroese fishing schooner *Stella Marie*. Coxswain Jeffrey Wright and Motor Mechanic Sydney Hill were awarded the Silver Medal from the R.N.L.I. and each crew member received a Vellum Service Certificate.

Presentation of Silver medals and Vellum service certificates

Lifeboat *'Frederick H. Pilley'* (1935-1939)

Lifeboat *'Frederick H. Pilley'* arrived on station at Fleetwood on August 28th, 1935. She was a similar lifeboat to her predecessor as a 38 foot self-righting lifeboat and was built in 1920 for the Lizard lifeboat station. She had been provided out of a gift from Mr F. H. Pilley, of Upper Norwood, in London.

With similar design and construction to the previous one she was driven by a single 45 horse power Tylor petrol-engine. She had greater horse-power engine with 45 horse power. instead of the 35 horse power of the previous lifeboat, giving a top speed of 7.5 knots.

Lifeboat *Frederick H. Pilley*

The *Frederick H. Pilley* lifeboat was 38 feet long with a 9 foot beam. She was built twenty five years earlier and was first stationed at The Lizard, Cornwall, before going to Port Askaig on Islay, in the Scottish Hebrides, as the first lifeboat on this new station. From this station she was shortly afterwards taken to Sandbank boatyard in the Clyde, where she was refurbished ready to be transferred to Fleetwood. This lifeboat was brought to Fleetwood by sea, crewed by Coxswain Jeffrey Wright and members of the Fleetwood Lifeboat Crew.

They left Sandbank at 09.30 a.m. on Monday morning in fine weather and arrived at Girvan at 16.30 p.m. the same day. On the following morning they left Girvan at 07.00 a.m. and reached Ramsey, Isle of Man at 18.30 p.m. They departed Ramsey Isle of Man at 8.00 a.m. on Wednesday morning and reached Fleetwood the same night around 17.30 p.m. The lifeboat was bedecked with heather to show she had come down from Scotland.

November 14th, 1936 Steamer *J & J Monks*

On Saturday 14th November 1936 the steam coaster *J & J Monks* left Fleetwood bound for Weston Point on the River Mersey, near Runcorn, with a cargo of gravel. At first all went well but engine trouble soon developed. Before they reached Lune Light the problems with the engine had worsened and they were making little headway. A boiler leak was preventing the engineers from maintaining steam pressure and it was necessary to shut down the boiler. With an onshore wind and strong tidal current Captain Reynolds decided to anchor until they could sort out the engine problem. The anchors failed to do any more than check their drift towards the coast and in progressively shallower water the waves were starting to break over the bows. In the darkness the captain knew they were off Cleveleys, being pushed towards the shore. The captain decided to burn distress flares to request assistance.

Around 20.45 p.m. that night the lifeboat maroons were fired to summon the crew and the lifeboat *Frederick H. Pilley* was launched to search for the coaster. The initial information was that watchers on Blackpool North Pier had seen distress signal around three miles north-west of Blackpool. The lifeboat having searched the reported area for an hour without seeing anything returned to the Fleetwood North End jetty around 23.00 p.m. The coxswain reported that they had not seen anything in the areas where the distressed vessel was reported to be. In the meantime people on shore had been able to see the steamer in distress and give bearings from the shore that fixed the position.

This was in the age before wireless communication and on arriving at the North End further information was given that the vessel was believed to be further offshore between Blackpool and Cleveleys and in the vicinity of the North-West Boulders, which is further out to sea off Rossall Point. At once the lifeboat turned around and proceeded seaward to resume the search. The lifeboat located the steamer and found her to be the *J&J Monks.* She was in shallow water and still afloat.

With the lifeboat alongside in readiness to take a tow, if required, the engineers on the steamer again prepared to stoke the leaking boiler. They had made a temporary repair to two rivets that had been leaking water and steam and they needed to raise steam to enable the anchors to be recovered.

Four hours had now passed since they had sent distress signals but with steam pressure raised and accompanied by the lifeboat the anchors were recovered. With the engineers 'coaxing the old girl along as best they could' the steamer gradually proceeded into deeper water. Only slow progress was made and it took a further four hours before the *J&J Monks*, under her own steam, limped into Fleetwood accompanied by the lifeboat. The lifeboat had been at sea for eight hours standing by the vessel as she returned to port with all on board safe.

Re-housing the lifeboat *Frederick H. Pilley*

Breasting ropes ready to manoeuvre onto slipway

Record of Service Rendered by lifeboat *Frederick H. Pilley (1935-1939)*

September 24th, 1935. Vessel reported drifting. No vessel found. Launched a few hours later to reported vessel aground. Nothing found.

October 15th, 1935. Fishing vessel *Noel* of Lancaster, aground on Pilling Sands.

November, 14th, 1936. Steamer *J&J Monks* of Liverpool. Broken down 3 miles North West of Blackpool North Pier.

August 14th, 1937. Motor yacht *Skippool.*

July 3rd, 1938. Motorboat *Pastime.*

February 17th, 1939. Motorboat *Sister Pat* out of fuel driven aground on Pilling Sands.

5 LIFEBOAT *'ANN LETITIA RUSSELL'* (1939-1976)

In February 1939 a new motor lifeboat was placed on station at Fleetwood. She had been built at Messrs. Groves and Guttridge, in Cowes, Isle of Wight, at a cost of £6,634 provided from the legacy of the late Miss Ann Russell from Manchester. She was a 41 foot Watson class, non-self-righting lifeboat, driven by two 35 horse power Weyburn AE6 petrol engines. This gave this boat a faster speed than her two predecessors, with a top speed of nearly 8 knots. At a service of dedication on 26th July, 1939, she was named by Lady Stanley as *'Ann Letitia Russell.'* In 1963, after almost 25 years of service, she was taken for a major re-fit, during which her original petrol engines were replaced by twin 47 horse power Parsons 'Porbeagle' diesel engines.

Motor lifeboat *Ann Letitia Russell*

One of the most famous rescues in the Fleetwood RNLI story came during World War 2, one August afternoon in 1941. The weather was far from summery and the lifeboat-men watched anxiously from the promenade observing a vessel struggling with the elements in the anchorage area west of Wyre Light.

Ann Letitia Russell lifeboat   Artist Ken Frost

She was the 300-ton three-masted schooner *Stella Marie* from Klaksvik, near Thorshaven, in the Faroe Islands, loaded to the gunwhales with fish. With the Humber ports closed down, Fleetwood had become Britain's main fishing port. Some trawlers and trawlermen were on naval duties as minesweepers and on convoy escort but others braved the U-boats and the mines to carry on fishing.

Their catches were vital food supplies in beleaguered Britain. Fish was never rationed but its distribution was controlled by the government and extra supplies shipped in from the Faroes and from Iceland were very welcome.

The lifeboat-men knew that *Stella Marie* was in trouble but Admiralty officials, based at the North Euston Hotel, refused permission for a rescue mission earlier in the day.

Stella Marie 1941

Stella Marie had sails and an engine but the fishermen reckoned that with the wind and tide conditions that morning they could have sailed the schooner up the channel to safety 'under bare poles' without the use of canvas or diesel fuel.

By the time the rescue was given official clearance, Coxswain Jeffrey Wright and his men knew they were facing a tough task. Now, *Stella Marie* was hard aground with huge seas breaking over her.

Coming alongside the stranded vessel *Ann Letitia Russell* was nearly overwhelmed. A mighty wave smashed her against the *Stella Marie* and swung her through 180 degrees. She was badly damage but all eight crew from the stricken vessel were snatched from the jaws of death and the lifeboat-men managed to get home safely.

Because the steering gear had been damaged in the rescue the control of the twin engines played a vital part. For that reason, motor mechanic Syd Hill, the only full-time member of the station team, received a Silver Medal alongside Coxswain Jeffrey Wright.

Coxswain Jeffrey Wright and crew following rescue from *Stella Marie*
photo courtesy of Lancashire County Council Red Rose Collections

Lifeboat crew with Coxswain Jeff Wright outside Boathouse
Photograph courtesy of Lancashire County Council Red Rose Collections

Wellington Bomber Aircraft crash 3th April, 1945.

A serious air accident happened off Fleetwood on Friday 13th April, 1945, when a Wellington bomber on a training exercise with trainee wireless operators crashed into the sea in front of the Marine Hall and five of the seven crew died.

Wellington Bomber

A Fleetwood dock worker Mr. Richard Hargreaves saw the plane flying low over the Mount Pavilion and narrowly missing the dome of the Marine Hall building as it skimmed low overhead. The bomber crashed into the sea around two hundred and fifty yards from the lower promenade. The weather was fine with a light southerly wind and calm sea. The tide was coming in and the sandbanks were covered with a few feet of water. Although the fuselage was beneath the surface the tail fin was sticking out of the water and a survivor was clinging to it, signalling for help. As Mr. Hargreaves ran to the Mount Hotel to call the police another observer further along the promenade Mr. Joseph Scott of 7, Avon Green went to assist. He had just finished a night shift working on Fleetwood Dock and was walking home along the promenade. He ran down to the beach and after taking off his clothes he plunged into the sea from a point opposite the former open-air swimming pool. As he was swimming he saw another man, who he later found to be a Canadian Air Force officer Jack Haley, swimming strongly towards the wrecked aircraft. As Mr. Hargreaves arrived his leg struck a piece of submerged wreckage and the Canadian reached the survivor first. They saw another survivor but he had already got into an inflatable life-raft and he was being swept eastward by the incoming tide. Both swimmers supported the man in the water and moved slowly towards the shore. They were wary of the strong currents in the deep water channel known as 'The Neckings' and took care to avoid being swept along the main River Wyre channel.

The three were spotted by Thomas Riches in the Prawner *White Heather*, that was outward bound from the Jubilee Quay, Fleetwood. He had seen the incident and came to the rescue, pulling the three people up onto the Prawner. Mr Hargreave's shin was cut and bruised from striking the wreckage. The *White Heather* then went to assist the survivor in the inflatable liferaft and took him onto their vessel.

Wing and wrecked fuselage photo Evening Gazette

At the Lifeboat Station when the message was received the coxswain and a number of other crew members were known to be at sea in the good weather, so to save time station mechanic Syd Hill gathered a scratch crew consisting of an Able Seaman from the Naval Reserve, two United States Army Corporals and a civilian visitor. The *Ann Letitia Russell* was launched at 11.10 a.m. and within ten minutes had reached the crash site where wreckage was floating on the surface. They talked to those on the *White Heather* and heard that there had been seven crew on the aircraft and the lifeboat searched the area for other survivors. By noon it was believed that a thorough search of the area had been completed and nothing was found of the other crewmen in the vicinity of the wreck at that time.

Tailplane section photo Evening Gazette

The survivors on board the *White Heather* were landed at Fleetwood and taken to Fleetwood Hospital where they were treated for their injuries. They were later transferred to Weeton Camp hospital.

The crash investigation report indicates that there were no mechanical defects and it was thought that whilst flying low a left hand turn over the sea had caused the wing tip to hit the water and roll the aircraft upside down as it crashed into the sea. The tail of the aircraft was around 100 yards away from the main fuselage and wings that were upside down on the sandbanks. Four of the bodies of the crew members were recovered from inside the aircraft when the tide went out leaving the wreckage on the sandbanks. They were carried ashore to a point opposite the Mount Hotel where they were placed in RAF vehicles.

James Leadbetter coxswain 1948 - 1953

When Jeff Wright retired as Coxswain in 1948 his place was taken by another inshore fisherman, James Leadbetter who had the nickname 'Fillocks'.

He served until December, 1953. When James Leadbetter retired he was honoured at a ceremony in the Fleetwood Town Hall on Queens Terrace – now the home of Fleetwood Museum and just round the corner from his home in Kent Street. The Mayor at the time was John Robinson, a fish merchant and prominent figure in the dockland world. He handed over a Certificate of Service from the Institution marking 20 years in lifeboats by James who had been both Second Coxswain and Bowman - an historic office given to man who acted like a Boatswain – a supervisor providing a link between crew and officers.

The Mayor recalled that, in 1949, James had been awarded the R.N.L.I. Bronze Medal for Gallantry.

It came from a notable double service – to the same casualty twice in 24 hours in April that year.

The 71-foot ketch *Alpha* had both sails and engine and was making a passage from Stranraer when she got into difficulties on the North Wharf sandbank. It was mid-afternoon and Coxswain Leadbetter found the Alpha bumping over the sands. Huge seas were running and the ketch was often lifted up much higher than the cockleshell lifeboat. But, despite the violent motion of both craft, eight people were rescued including a boy of 10.

Lifeboat Coxswain James Leadbetter

When the tide went out it left the *Alpha* high and dry and six of the crew decided to walk out to her. They were warned of the dangers by the Coastguards and by Coxswain Leadbetter but ignored the advice.

By morning there was no sign of the *Alpha*. Once again the lifeboatmen risked their lives and started a search in seas whipped up by what was now a full gale. They found the *Alpha* aground on the Clarke's Wharf sandbank and powered in through a mass of white water to snatch the six men to safety.

Coxswain Leadbetter's courage and skilled seamanship was honoured by his Bronze medal and the station secretary, local dentist Bert Cartman, received a Letter of Appreciation for stepping in on the first service to act as assistant mechanic. Anecdotally, 'Jimmy' Leadbetter was the hottest man in London on the day this photograph was taken, because he was dressed in this outfit on a Summer day for the medal presentation.

In 1954 both Jeff Wright and James Leadbetter joined a group of Fleetwood people who took part in an unusual survey.

It was conducted by local man Peter Wright B.A., who was researching a thesis for the degree of Doctor of Philosophy in the Department of English Language and Medieval History at the University of Leeds.

Mr Wright, whose father William had skippered the Fleetwood – Knott End ferry, produced an extremely detailed and learned work which is now enshrined in two handsomely hard-backed volumes titled: A Grammar of the Dialect of Fleetwood (Lancashire) Descriptive and Historical.

He interviewed witnesses from various walks of life to provide information about traditional names used for a vast range of everyday things from fish to parts of a boat and how they were pronounced. Today, the thesis provides a fascinating insight into the world of sailing craft and into aspects of everyday life in and around Fleetwood in far off times.

There was one memory which stayed clear in Jeff's mind all through his long life. He was only a toddler when that terrible storm lashed the Lancashire coast in November 1890 and many lives were lost.

"I had been staying at my grand-parents house and I remember waking up one morning and realising that everything was very quiet after the roaring of the wind had died down. I went downstairs and the house was deserted so I went into the back yard and there were my grandparents with the body of their son who had been drowned. He lay on the flags in the back yard and they were washing him so that he could be brought inside and laid out properly for his funeral."

No fewer than 10 seafarers had lost their lives around Morecambe Bay that day.

Perhaps it was just a coincidence that a body was recovered from the sea on the day of Coxswain Wright's own funeral.

Herbert Rawcliffe coxswain 1954

Tragedy struck Fleetwood lifeboat station one bitter February night in 1954.

Just five weeks after he was appointed Coxswain following 30 years experience as a lifeboat-man, inshore fisherman Herbert Rawcliffe lost his life at sea.

Coxswain James Leadbetter *(left)* and Coxswain Herbert Rawcliffe

He was also a pilot whose job was to guide visiting cargo ships in and out of the port.

Just before midnight that Saturday night he was one of four men who sailed out into Morecambe Bay onboard the Prawner *Eleanora* which had been chartered because the regular pilot boat, *Robin*, had engine trouble. There was a near gale-force wind, sleet and snow were falling and there was a heavy swell. Skipper Arthur Swales brought his little craft alongside the Dutch coaster *Bon Aire* which was carrying a cargo of carbide for the ICI factory up river at Thornton. Crewman Reg Salthouse, who normally commanded the *Robin*, told journalists later: "It was a shocking night. I never remember it being so pitch-black. Mr Rawcliffe got hold of the *Bon Aire's* rail and had one foot in the scuppers ready to climb aboard when the *Eleanora* seemed to heave away and he slipped and lost his grip and fell into the sea between the two craft."

It was not until August of that year that the veteran sailor was returned by the sea. His body was washed up at Rossall Beach and identified from a pocket watch – and by the fact that he always wore his navy blue lifeboat jersey so that the red embroidered letters R.N.L.I. were at the back.

At the inquest a verdict of misadventure was recorded on the 54-year-old lifeboat-men after dramatic evidence from his friend and colleague Albert Wright who succeeded him as Coxswain. He said the *Bon Aire* was anchored in Heysham Lake – the upper reaches of Lune Deeps - but no one answered when the *Eleanora* approached the ship and hailed her. After Mr Rawcliffe slipped in the icy conditions and fell in they saw him near the stern of the coaster. He called out several times.

Mr Wright said his friend was one of the best swimmers he had ever seen but it was very cold. "We saw him in the light of a deck-lamp about 20 feet to windward of us. We could just see his head above the water." The *Eleanora* party threw a line which fell just short. The second attempt saw the rope fall over Mr Rawcliffe's shoulder. " He made no attempt to grab at these lines, " said Mr Wright. " We stood by with a boathook to grab him but the swell washed him away and that was the last we saw of him."

Mrs Rawcliffe told the County Coroner, William Blackhurst, that her husband was a healthy man but he was very tired when he left that night for his pilotage duties.

The inquest heard that he had been out in the lifeboat for six hours earlier in the day. In the five weeks since he took over as Coxswain there had been two major incidents in very bad conditions.

First came the loss of the Prawner *Florence Baxter* which Mr Rawcliffe owned. He was not onboard at the time but the man who was on-board lost his life. Then, a week later an RAF Washington bomber with seven men onboard came down in Morecambe Bay in freezing cold and heavy snow. The bomber search, which yielded nothing, was the biggest combined operation then seen in the area. It involved six lifeboats, trawlers, naval ships and aircraft. Lasting more than 16 hours, this was the longest service performed by a Fleetwood lifeboat and they only returned as fuel ran low. The twin engines had burned 100 gallons of petrol. After snatching some hot food, the crew were back at the boathouse in less than an hour expecting to resume the search. However, they were stood down as hopes of finding anyone alive quickly faded.

Hours after Mr Rawcliffe's death, news of the tragedy spread through the port and prayers were offered in local churches by local people visibly affected by the tragedy.

At the age of 20 Mr. Rawcliffe had been awarded the Meritorious Service Medal for his work in the Royal Naval Reserve in the 1914-18 war.

He did gallant rescue work in the Fleetwood flood of 1927.

He and Hilda had no children of their own but his nephews played a big part in his life.

Like other Fleetwood youngsters, the six Rawcliffe boys were always playing around the Jubilee Quay. Two of them – Bill and Alec – sometimes took their uncle's prawner *Florence Baxter* on fishing trips when he was busy with pilotage duties. Bill remembers: "We used to follow Cush Wright and fish where he went. He told us: I wish I had a dog as faithful as you."

It was a grim coincidence that the Prawner Florence Baxter also became a victim of the sea only weeks before her owner. The little craft was wrecked in an incident which cost the life of Richard Wright of Blakiston Street who was alone onboard in January 1954.

It was a chapter in a sea saga which began one stormy day in 1940. A brand-new prawner, *Capella*, was on passage to Fleetwood from the builders in Conway, North Wales. Onboard was the skipper, John 'Judy' Wright and his son Harry. They ran aground approaching the King Scar area in misty conditions when the wartime blackout meant no shore lights. The boat was smashed to bits in the heavy seas. Both men lost their lives just a mile from shore.

At that time, Harry's brother Richard was serving in the Royal Navy. But, 14 years later to the day, he was working the *Florence Baxter* alone and ran aground in roughly the same place – a mile south south east of King Scar buoy.

The weather had turned stormy and the owner of the *Florence Baxter*, Herbert Rawcliffe, grew concerned when he learned that Richard had gone out alone. Days of bad weather had prevented the inshore fleet from fishing and Richard's regular crewmate had left for a job in a distant water trawler.

Newly appointed as lifeboat Coxswain, Herbert raised the alarm and a four hour search in rough seas began which ended when the *Florence Baxter's* mast was seen half out of the water. The boat was wrecked and there was no sign of the lone fisherman.

The trilogy of tragedy ended just a few weeks later when Herbert lost his own life in the waters of Morecambe Bay.

Years later, his nephew, Bill Rawcliffe became Second Coxswain at Fleetwood and his great nephew, Will Rawcliffe, a crew member.

Albert Wright coxswain 1954 – 1960

Albert Wright was appointed as coxswain in February 1954 and retired in 1960. It was on the death of his friend and fellow Pilot Herbert Rawcliffe that he became coxswain. He was born in 1900 and died in 1963. His father was a fisherman from Marshside, on the Northern fringe of Southport.

Like many Wright's the family moved to Fleetwood in 1908, bringing their 36 foot long 'half-decker' *"Hannah"* (FD225). Albert himself was always connected with the sea, and became one of Fleetwood's harbour pilots. He lived in Arthur Street, very close to the lifeboat-house and served on the lifeboat for many years. He was involved in over 200 emergency launches. On the 8th June, 1955, he was coxswain of the

Lifeboat Coxswain Albert Wright

Ann Letitia Russell lifeboat when the Manx steamer *Mona's Isle* ran aground in the River Wyre following a collision with the inshore fishing vessel *Ludo*. The lifeboat took 153 passengers off the Mona's Isle but sadly one of the two fishermen on the *Ludo* lost his life.

Albert was also one of the pioneers of the Fleetwood Model Yacht Club.

Richard (Cush) Wright succeeded Albert Wright and was appointed coxswain in 1960 following Albert Wright's retirement.

Fleetwood Lifeboat Crew circa 1955

Fleetwood lifeboat crew (circa 1955) Left to right - John McDonough (Ginger John), Coxswain Albert Wright, Jack Salthouse, Mechanic Syd Hill, Richard Wright, Clyde Salthouse and Ronnie Hooper.

Richard (Cush) Wright coxswain 1960 – 1964.

Lifeboat Coxswain Richard 'Cush' Wright

Richard Wright was a true Old Man of the Sea.

He was just 13 years old when he started work as crewman on his father's fishing craft, *Agnes*. Even at that young age he was already no stranger to the maritime world having been around boats since he was old enough to walk.

Richard stayed afloat as an inshore fisherman until he was turned 80 years old stating that at age 65 he was working as hard as he had ever done.

His record as a lifeboat-man was an equally proud one.

He joined the crew at the age of 17 and served for more than 44 years. He was Coxswain between 1960 and 1964 and took part in many epic rescues over the years.

Dick (Cush) Wrights Prawner in Jubilee Quay *Judy (FD212)*

(Illustrated above is Dick Wrights inshore fishing boat, the Prawner *Judy* (FD212) in the Jubilee Quay, Fleetwood).

Although Fleetwood became the third biggest UK fishing port with ships that brought catches from grounds off Iceland, Greenland, Norway and Russia as well as Britain's western seaboard and the coast of Ireland, there was always a fleet of inshore fishing vessels that operated in Morecambe Bay and the eastern Irish Sea.

A traditional part of the fleet were the Prawners – also known as Half-Deckers or Nobbies. Some have survived as yachts. Richard Wright was brought up in these boats and in the community that traced its roots to the banks of the Ribble near Southport. So many had the surname Wright that nicknames were needed to identify them in conversation.

Dick was Cush Wright like his father and though he did not know the origin he had been told: " There's Young Cush and Old Cush and Old Cush's son. Young Cush will be Old Cush when Old Cush's done." He knew the origin was in the bible – Cush was the grandson of Noah and father of Nimrod the Hunter which is apt for a fisherman.

Others included: Skylight, Spuddy Dick and Dickie Dipple. Like many of the Wrights, Dick attended Mount Road Methodist Church as a boy though not in later life. He described himself as: "A believer." Dick came across as a patient, unflappable man who didn't use seamanlike language. He loved to play snooker and billiards in leisure time and to visit the cinema. He was the father of two daughters and two sons who were both seafarers.

Long years of experience gave him a picture of Morecambe Bay in his head like a modern-day electronic map. Interviewed nearly 40 years ago he said: " I have never seen a chart. Give me a clock, a depth sounder and a compass and I will take you anywhere you want to go."

From the days of sail and oars in both fishing vessels and lifeboats, Dick saw many changes – not always for the better. He blamed an increasing use of household detergents in raw sewage then discharged to the sea for the huge decline in the shrimp population off the Lancashire Coast and he was concerned that modern, more powerful boats with more efficient fishing gear were taking too much from the stocks.

A very successful fisherman, Dick used to say: " You can have a good day but our boats and our nets leave a bit for tomorrow." His Prawner, *Judy*, is preserved at Fleetwood Museum.

Like many traditional fisherman, Dick never learned to swim but he survived several accidents which put him in the water. A 12 hour shift of hard physical work was the norm and he was no stranger to being wet through.

The little money paid to the crews was important in the early days. "We got 25p for a practice turnout and it was first to the boathouse who got it. I've seen a single man give his place to a married man because he knew he needed that five bob."

Dick knew the sea in all its moods. "In bad weather it's knowing the boat and how to handle it. I'm not frightened of the sea – I respect it. You've got to respect it. It's as though it's alive – not as a person but it's like a living thing."

Richard's father, William, who had spent his early life at sea as an inshore fisherman, later took a job on the fish docks. He was Coxswain from 1923 to 1933 but served the RNLI for many years afterwards assisting at the lifeboat station. He died in 1945 after he was injured in an accident at the boathouse involving the winch used to draw the lifeboat back up the sloping slipway into the boathouse.

Ben Bee coxswain 1964- 1969

Ben Bee was one of three Fleetwood brothers who all earned a living from the sea. Like his brother Kenneth, he lost his life to the waters.

Lifeboat Coxswain Ben Bee

The three men grew up in a family where money was in short supply. Their father had been a prisoner of war during World War 1 and the harsh conditions he endured left him suffering from tuberculosis, which claimed his life in the 1920's.

Ben's brother Frank Bee sailed as a trawlerman from Fleetwood as a youngster and served in the Royal Navy during World War 2. He came ashore to work in the world of wholesale fish and spent years living in the south of England while he worked at the famous Billingsgate market in London.

But he never lost touch with the sea and had a small boat built for him in which he used to go angling off the south coast.

Later, back in Fleetwood, he was a mobile fish retailer and operated charter boats taking angling parties into Morecambe Bay. He was very successful and, in retirement, kept up his boat angling hobby.

Brother Kenneth also worked on charter boats and was drowned in the river Wyre where his craft was kept on a mooring in the area known as 'back of the dock'. He often went to and from the boat alone in a small dinghy and suffered a fatal accident when he fell overboard. His body was recovered and he was buried in Fleetwood cemetery.

Ben Bee joined the inshore fishing fleet at the Jubilee Quay and worked for some years as skipper of the Prawner *Annie*. Later he became a partner in one of the country's oldest fishing vessels, the little inshore trawler *Biddy* of which he was the skipper.

Ben became coxswain of Fleetwood lifeboat in 1964 at a time when leisure sailing was on the increase, which lead to increased work for the lifeboat crews' along with more incidents involving bathers, wind-surfers and youngsters on air beds.

In the summer of 1966 Fleetwood received its first " inshore rescue boat" which was ideal for dealing with many of these incidents close to the shore in shallow waters.

Typical of the inshore fishermen who had served Fleetwood lifeboat so well, Ben was a very competent seaman with a lot of local knowledge. He was a laid-back character, a kindly man with a ready smile, and not cast in the Captain Bligh mould.

During his service as Coxswain, which ended in 1969, Ben and his men encountered a series of bizarre hoax calls which occurred at intervals between 1964 and 1966. The culprit was never found.

David Pearce interviewed Ben in 1987 for the documentary film *White Socks and Telemacs*, which covered some aspects of Fleetwood's story ashore and afloat and for which he wrote the script.

Ben recalled: " We could not ignore these radio calls so we had to go out. The worst one meant we spent 12 hours at sea in very bad weather searching for a Belgian trawler that was supposed to be in trouble three miles west of where the old Morecambe Bay Lightship used to be. The hoax calls were always late at night – early in the morning – and always when it was blowing. That was the worst one I remember."

On another occasion, in August 1964, the Fleetwood and Barrow lifeboats spent six hours at sea in very heavy weather after a radio message was picked up by the coastguard. It was supposed to be a Mayday distress call from the Fleetwood inshore fishing boat *Teal*.

Communications were very different in those days from today's sophisticated radio telephones and computer systems and it was not until late that night that the *Teal* was found – safely berthed in Whitehaven harbour.

Looking back on his service Ben recalled: "I had every confidence in the boat, in the crew, and in myself." It was a job, he chuckled: " someone had to do it!"

Like many fishermen, Ben was a snappy dresser when he took his wife Winnie out for the evening and complained that he had several good suits, shirts and shoes destroyed by seawater on lifeboat services.

In 1994 Ben was skipper of the inshore boat *Scipio,* which capsized during the operation of the fishing gear. He and his crewman found themselves in the water very quickly but they were picked up by the Barrow lifeboat. Sadly, Ben could not be revived although his shipmate survived.

Later, Ben's ashes were scattered on the waters he knew so well in a ceremony on-board the Fleetwood lifeboat *William Street.*

Fleetwood Lifeboat Crew circa 1969

Fleetwood lifeboat crew (circa 1969) Back row left to right – John McDonough (Ginger John), Honorary Secretary Dick Willoughby, Second Coxswain Noel Bird, Norman Pendlebury, Mechanic Brian Gerrard, Roy Mitchinson, Boathouse Attendant Joe Dyer. Front row – District Engineer Stan Brett, Lifeboat Inspector Cdr. Harold Harvey, Coxswain Ben Bee and Head Launcher Barrie Farmer.

Roy Mitchinson coxswain 1969 - 1976

Coxswain Roy Mitchinson was born in 1930 and served an apprenticeship as a motor mechanic. After two years National Service in the army he returned to Fleetwood and became a deep sea fishermen working in the engine room where he qualified as a chief engineer.

Lifeboat Coxswain Roy Mitchinson

In 1958 he joined the inshore fishing industry and in 1965 he bought the prawner *Hannah Hambleton* which he re-engined with a Parsons Porbeagle diesel engine – the same power unit as the Ann Letitia Russell now had.

Roy and his wife had two sons and a daughter and his son Gary became a successful inshore fisherman, as his father had done. Gary sold his trawler – *Albion* - in 2016 and took a job ashore on the docks because the economics of the industry were no longer viable.

Roy, who served for a time as Chairman of the Fleetwood Inshore Fishermens Association, was appointed Coxswain in 1969 and served until 1975 when he had to stand down because new eyesight regulations had been introduced by the R.N.L.I. and he was unable to pass the colour-blindness test. The same applied to his deputy, Noel Bird.

It was a tough call for them both, especially Roy who had devoted himself so much to the R.N.L.I. service that he neglected his own fishing business at times although he was not the only inshore fisherman who lost money through his lifeboat service.

Roy achieved national fame when he became the face of the R.N.L.I. Although his portrait was anonymous his rugged profile and strong jaw were seen all over the country on posters.

A former member of the Fleetwood Sea Cadet Corps as a youth where he played in the prize-winning band, Roy was one of the originators of the highly-successful Sea Cadet Old Boys Band which has helped to raise thousands for charity.

Yacht Acco 25th July, 1970.

A particularly arduous service was undertaken on Saturday 25th July, 1970, when as dawn broke the lifeboat was called out on service. A vicious summer storm had been raging overnight with severe gale force 9 winds rattling rooftops across the town of Fleetwood in an unseasonal manner. When the Coastguard rang the Honorary Secretary of Fleetwood Lifeboat shortly before 5.00 a.m. it was already full daylight. A radio message had been received from the Morecambe Bay Light-Vessel, some 20 miles West of Fleetwood, informing the coastguard that a large converted fishing vessel, the *Acco*, was close by their position with the occupants shouting for help in the rough sea conditions that had built up overnight in the gale force conditions. The decision was quickly taken to launch the lifeboat and the Hon. Sec rang coxswain Roy Mitchinson relaying the message from the coastguard, telling him to 'bang em up" (fire the lifeboat maroons to summon the crew). As he hurriedly dressed, Roy's wife Doreen started ringing around the crew to say "callout". Roy was the first to arrive at the lifeboathouse, soon followed by Motor Mechanic Brian Gerrard. The mortar was dragged outside onto the Promenade and two maroons were fired.

With the light still cold and grey the boathouse came to life as crew members arrived in their cars, summoned by the telephone call or the maroons. They pushed through the narrow doorway past Bert Crossthwaite, the Winchman, who was preparing to set the winch cable ready for launching.

Roy had already donned his oilskins and lifejacket as other crewmen collected their oilskin jackets and leggings from the rack, along with their lifejacket. He heard the heavy boathouse doors swing back on their hinges and roll open as Head Launcher Barrie Farmer and his small team started to push back the doors on their rollers, giving a dull rumble, first one then the other clipped back to restrain them in readiness for launching.

The anorak jackets and trousers weren't easy to put on and with crew still donning their waterproof gear at various places around the deck the bow chocks were removed by the launchers and the lifeboat rocked forward from the resting position on its cradle to align itself on the slipway. The mechanic had completed his preparations to start the engines and waited for the coxswain to check that everyone was clear of the propellers before giving the order to 'start up'. Whilst waiting Coxswain Roy allowed his gaze to stray through the open doors ahead of him, down to the river below. In his mind he was double-checking his understanding of the tide time to decide whether there would be sufficient water in these conditions to go West through 'The Neckings' channel.

It was about an hour after high water and even at the bottom of the slipway the waves looked menacing in the gale force conditions. Within a minute all was ready. The aft chain had been released when the winchman had taken up the weight of the lifeboat on the winch cable. With one further glance all around to check everything was clear, it was time to launch. 'Standby' Roy called, the force of his authority pulling the crew to readiness. The order 'Knock out aft' quickly followed and Barrie Farmer, positioned under the stern of the lifeboat cradle swung his hammer to strike quick release shackle on the winch cable, releasing the last fetter that held the lifeboat at the top of the slipway. In an instant the lifeboat was free to commence its run down the slipway. As the lifeboat entered the water a bow wave threw spray across the crew on the foredeck who were already raising the hinged foremast to set up the aerial wires. The small mizzen mast was similarly erected and the locking fitting set in place.

Fleetwood lifeboat *Ann Letitia Russell* was launched at 05.12 a.m. with six crew on board, two less than the normal eight but it was felt necessary to get away quickly in the bad weather and not wait around for other crew to turn up. It was approximately an hour after high water and the coxswain assessed that there would be sufficient water through the inshore passage 'The Neckings' and headed along the shoreline in front of the promenade, rather than proceeding down the channel to Wyre Light. This was to save time in heading west-south-west towards the light-vessel. The seas were rough as the lifeboat proceeded towards Rossall Point and within another mile had become very rough, with fifteen foot breaking waves at the west end of 'The Neckings'.

The Coastguard on duty logged that the lifeboat was *'jumping clean out of the water'* as she passed their lookout station. The crew on board were realising how bad the weather would be for the next fifteen miles as they headed straight into the high seas whipped up by the north-west-by-west force 8-9 winds that had lashed the coast all night. One particular wave at this point sent the bow skyward and as the lifeboat passed over the crest of the wave both propellers raced as they left the water when the lifeboat tilted forward on the downward plunge. As the bow submerged the impact sent a shudder throughout the hull and the whiplash effect on the mast caused the long wire aerials to part and tumble down on the deck, preventing any communication until they could be re-hung. Breaking wave after breaking wave swept spray and solid water along the length of the deck. All six crew were sheltering beside the steering position behind the aft canopy. Time after time the water surged along the side-decks in such quantities that it threatened to overflow the cockpit coaming, potentially filling the canopy shelter deck with sea water. Second coxswain, Noel Bird, joined Roy Mitchinson at the helm to keep the boat steady on course in the mountainous seas.

As they cleared the coast the seas were less breaking but still extremely rough as mile after mile they doggedly proceeded at best speed towards the *Acco*, near Morecambe Bay Light Vessel. The crew were already soaked to the skin, as they were for the rest of their two hour outward journey. Brian Gerrard, the motor mechanic, managed to re-rig the radio aerial wire to re-establish communication on the 2MHz band. Every ten minutes or so the lifeboat took green seas on board that buried the bow and swept aft along the deck, causing each crew member to hang on tight as the water spilled through the scuppers and over the stern. For mile after mile the crew encountered seas unparalleled in their experience, until they arrived in the vicinity of Morecambe Bay Light-ship. In the adverse conditions it took until 07.15 a.m. before the light-ship was sighted and as the lifeboat drew close by the *Acco* could be seen to be lying astern of the light-ship, attached to a rope.

Rolling seas and breaking wave made the approach to get alongside the *Acco* dangerous. As Roy Mitchinson manoeuvered the lifeboat to get close alongside the *Acco* to assess the situation the breaking seas seemed to be getting worse. With the sea conditions being so difficult Noel Bird (second coxswain) adopted the unusual practice of standing at the other side of the wheel, facing aft so that with Roy at the wheel facing forward between them they could see any rogue waves approaching them from ahead or astern as they took a turn around the *Acco* to consider what best to do.

Although people could be seen in the wheelhouse on board the *Acco* no-one ventured on deck to assist in taking a rope or attempted communication with the lifeboat. Earlier radio contact between the light-vessel and the lifeboat had reported there were 2 men and 1 woman on board and they were all very sea-sick and exhausted. Roy quickly recognised that those on board were unlikely to be able to assist in setting up a tow, so he decided to put Noel Bird on board to assist. At times like this you need to have confidence in the capability of the person you send across to the casualty to be able to take charge of the situation and be able to sort things out in the unpredictable scenario they are likely to encounter.

Coxswain Roy assessed the situation and realised this would be a stern test of his seamanship. The iron hulled light-vessel lay to a heavy chain attached to its bow and was facing into the waves, giving an unusual and slow pitching motion. The *Acco* was tied astern of the light-vessel and itself facing into the waves, so Roy knew that he would be unable to find any shelter in the lee of either the *Acco* or the light-vessel when he needed Noel to jump across to the *Acco*.

Morecambe Bay Light Vessel photo Stephen Musgrave

(Pictured above is Morecambe Bay light vessel on a different occasion in good weather conditions.)

Noel Bird

Approaching from astern of the *Acco*, Roy briefed his crew that he would go in near to the *Acco* again, to gauge the state of the seas but not transfer Noel at this point. Rope fenders were dragged from their stowage position under the for'ard canopy and set down the port side of the lifeboat. Large cresting waves were hitting the bows of the lifeboat and throwing water right along the deck as they slowly inched alongside. For all his daring Roy didn't want to risk serious damage to the lifeboat by remaining alongside and even though they were only feet away from the *Acco* no-one emerged. Having passed along the starboard side of the *Acco*, on clearing the *Acco's* bow Roy turned the lifeboat around again in a large clockwise circle and told Noel to standby to transfer at the next pass. The crew dragged the tow-rope from under the for'ard canopy and along the port side-deck, taking a turn around the aft towing bits then out over the stern and back over the guard chain rail, leaving enough rope to flake down in zig-zag lengths up and down the port deck. Noel set up a heaving line, attaching one end of it to the lifeboat's tow-rope and coiled the remainder to take with him.

As Roy shouted above the wind to those on the fore-deck that he was turning to commence his run-in to the *Acco,* Noel went along the deck to release upper part of the mid-ships chain-rail gate along the lifeboat's side to allow him to step through the gap and across onto the *Acco.* Two crew, Sandy McPherson and Norman Pendlebury, flanked Noel Bird on the port side-deck in a place just ahead of the mid-ships position. This steadied Noel as he prepared to jump across to board the *Acco,* with the heaving line. Seagulls wheeled and screeched above them as though they too were alarmed at what was about to happen. The *Acco* was pitching to the seas, plunging its bow one moment and rearing up alarmingly the next. Roy shouted quick instructions to the crew on deck as he turned the wheel to coax the lifeboat slowly alongside. The lifeboat was still plunging violently with each successive wave, making conditions truly difficult. Judgement was needed to find a moment when the two craft were pitching in phase.

Roy knew that split second timing would be necessary to get the lifeboat carefully alongside. Watchful for the menace of each tumbling sea, and with consummate skill Roy placed the port bow of the lifeboat alongside the starboard side of the *Acco.* He gave the starboard engine a quick kick astern to align the lifeboat alongside just long enough for Noel to shake off the support from his colleagues' arms as he judged the moment to step over the lower part of the chain rail gate and jump onto the starboard bulwark of the *Acco.* In a trice he was across the gap and with heaving line in hand - although landing heavily on the deck he was able to recover his balance, stepping forward towards the *Acco's* bow to prepare to make fast the tow-rope. The *Acco* had a bow roller for'ard and passing the heaving line outside the fitting and back to the deck cleat he was able to take a few figure of eight turns to secure the heaving line. Then unaided by anyone from the *Acco* he commenced pulling the heavy tow rope across from the lifeboat. Yard by yard the tow rope became heavier as he pulled more rope across and the task became strength sapping as he heaved with all his might to get enough length to enable the tow rope to be secured on the fore-deck fitting. Coxswain Roy had slowly eased the lifeboat forward to position her clear of the *Acco's* bow, allowing the tow-rope to be slowly paid out, whilst also maintaining a safe distance from the light-vessel's hull. The crewmen of the light-vessel were gathered at its stern observing the proceedings and preparing to release the rope that still tethered the *Acco* to the light-vessel.

The life-boat tow-rope was secured on the *Acco's* bow fixing and with just a hand signal from Noel on the *Acco* the light-vessel crew understood this command to release the *Acco* from their stern, allowing the lifeboat to take up the tow in preparation to head back to Fleetwood. It was now 07.45 a.m. The wind was still north-westerly and with 20 foot waves all those on board both the *Ann Letitia Russell* lifeboat and the *Acco* knew they were in for an uncomfortable few hours. As the Morecambe Bay light-vessel receded into the distance the skies looked ever threatening and the gale force conditions persisted. The breaking waves were striking the port quarter of both vessels, causing an unpleasant roll that made steering difficult. Noel, in the wheelhouse of the *Acco*, took the helm to aim for the stern of the lifeboat in an attempt to follow the tow but the high sides of the *Acco* were continuously buffeted by the wind, which caused the *Acco* to veer off course, putting strain on the tow. The three adults, two men and one woman, were slumped in the corner of the wheelhouse completely exhausted by their ordeal and suffering from severe sea-sickness. After the first ten minutes under tow Noel used a short length of rope to lash the wheel in the mid-ships position to see if he could get below to look around and find drinking water to give to those on board.

As he descended the companionway stairs at the aft end of the wheelhouse – to his complete surprise he found a further three adults plus three children, some in the main cabin and others in the for'ard cabin bunks. Noel suddenly realized there were now 9 people on board plus himself. Those below decks were in the same exhausted and nauseous condition and he quickly talked to two of the adults who explained they had been on a trip from Barrow-in-Furness to Douglas, Isle-of-Man, but the weather had turned nasty and the engine kept stopping due to a suspected fuel blockage. Having seen the three children lying prostrate on the bunks he expressed concern for their condition but the adults said they were doing their best to look after them in the difficult circumstances.

In the galley Noel took the kettle from the gimbaled cooker and filled it with cold water from the tap. Picking up a couple of mugs from the sink he struggled back up the stairs clutching the kettle and mugs. As he got halfway up the stairs and before he emerged into the wheelhouse a large sea hit the *Acco* causing her to heel over at an alarming angle. From somewhere below he could hear items tumbling and crashing around as the *Acco* rolled to the wave. He managed to keep hold of the kettle and mugs and as the *Acco* came back upright he released his grip on the handrail and climbed the remaining steps to enter the wheelhouse. Two of the three people in the wheelhouse were slumped in the corner on the starboard side but one man was on his feet steadying himself against the continuous rolling of their vessel. Noel offered him a cup of water and insisted he should encourage the other two to also have a drink.

The fact that there were nine people on the *Acco* concerned Noel and he went down from the wheelhouse and out through the starboard access door onto the side deck, bracing himself as he moved forward towards the bow. Steadying himself on the forestay he waved both arms to indicate he needed to communicate with the lifeboat. Coxswain Roy saw the signal and told Dave Scott and Norman Pendlebury to prepare to shorten the tow rope, pulling the slack on board the lifeboat as Roy reduced engine speed to let the *Acco* come closer. He didn't want to get too close under the conditions because of the risk of the *Acco* striking the lifeboat. At first it was impossible to hear Noel's shouts above the wind and engine noise but a combination of Noel raising all his fingers, while bending one thumb and shouting again made those on board the lifeboat understand there were 9 persons plus the second coxswain on-board the *Acco*.

Roy considered the options and briefly contemplated transferring everyone on to the lifeboat but the risks were extreme in the severe weather conditions. He instructed Brian Gerrard, the mechanic, to communicate to the coastguard their understanding that there were nine persons on board the *Acco* and also state that having considered the situation he had decided to continue the tow towards Fleetwood with all persons remaining on board the *Acco*. Having let those on the lifeboat know how many persons were on the *Acco* Noel checked the tow-rope fastening on the fore-deck before carefully walking aft to the wheelhouse as the lifeboat once again took up the tow. Re-gaining his position at the wheel Noel had a good look around the horizon before releasing the lashing from the wheel and attempting to steer the *Acco* in line astern of the lifeboat. There was no noticeable improvement in the weather conditions as the wind remained at gale force 8, gusting severe gale force 9, but the visibility had increased to around five miles. Noel chatted to one man in the wheelhouse who was standing up, to get a clearer understanding of what had happened. He then asked the man to go below to check on the six people in the main cabin and make sure they had a good drink of water.

Albeit slowly the tow seemed to be alright and from his position at the wheel Noel reached beneath his oilskin jacket into his pocket to get his pipe. It seemed that no sooner than he had lit his pipe and taken a deep inward breath that a large wave lifted the port quarter alarmingly, once again causing the *Acco* to veer off course. The tow-rope went bar-tight, shaking water droplets along its length with the strain and unable to support the increased load it parted close to the *Acco's* bow. The long tail of the tow-rope snaked upwards before falling back into the sea under its own weight. Those on board the lifeboat responded rapidly by pulling the slack rope back onto the lifeboats deck to prevent it fouling their propellers.

As the coxswain turned the lifeboat downwind in a large circle the crew worked on the frayed end of the tow-rope, putting a temporary seizing line around the three frayed parts of the rope to bind them together ready to use again. The heaving line was then attached to the end of the tow-rope in readiness to pass it back across to the *Acco*. Sandy McPherson set the rope fenders along the port side of the lifeboat and Roy brought the *'Ann Letitia'* back along the *Acco's* starboard side in preparation to re-connect the tow. Again Noel appeared alone on the foredeck ready to catch the heaving line. Dave Scott took the monkey's fist end in one hand and coiled the heaving line, separating it into two coils ready to throw. As the lifeboat passed along the *Acco's* side, about twenty feet away, without need for an order Dave judged the time to throw the line across and Noel caught it on-board the *Acco*. The tow-rope was once again dragged across and although it was energy sapping work the tow was made fast again. Noel immediately untied the heaving line and roughly coiling it he threw it back across to the stern of the lifeboat before it had moved too far away. Care was taken in paying out the tow-rope as the lifeboat's stern was rising and falling around ten feet as each wave passed under the stern. Although the whole process had taken time the tow was re-commenced.

Less than twenty minutes later the tow-rope parted again as another rogue wave threw the *Acco* wildly. With more than ten miles yet to go before they could expect any shelter in the Fleetwood channel Noel decided that in the extreme weather conditions he would use a car-tyre 'fender' from the *Acco* to buffer the tow. The line had parted around thirty feet from the *Acco's* bow so Noel pulled the tow-rope end back on board and clove hitched it around the tyre walls. He held up the car tyre as a signal to the lifeboat of his intention. This was immediately understood and the lifeboat was already closing with the *Acco* to pass the heaving line and tow-rope once again. Dave repeated his action in throwing the heaving line across and without difficulty Noel secured the tow-rope end on the opposite side of the tyre 'fender' as a shock absorber. He passed the tyre over the bow attached to the tow-rope and those on board the lifeboat eased the turns on the aft towing 'bitts' until the coxswain was satisfied with the length of the tow.

At first the tow seemed to be better with the tyre in place but with no improvement in the weather conditions and at times twenty foot high breaking waves the tow rope would go bar tight as the lifeboats stern lifted to a wave and the *Acco* with its tall masts disappeared from sight behind the wall of water that grew to separate them with its mountainous crest. It seemed only a matter of time before the tow would part again and Roy re-considered whether to take everyone off the *Acco* and abandon her. For a further twenty minutes the tow-rope held but when a particularly large wave threw the *Acco* off course the tension on the rope was simply too much and the tow-rope parted with a whip-lash 'crack' sound; the free-end recoiling back to the lifeboat with explosive force. Before anyone on board the lifeboat could react the tow-rope snaked towards them striking the stern with such force that it demolished the aft chain-rails and the mizzen mast. Only the protective rail behind the steering position prevented the coxswain being struck and injured as the rope curled back to land on-board the lifeboat.

Without the lifeboats tow the *Acco* was now wallowing broadside on to the sea and rolling alarmingly as wave after wave struck her hull. With considerable difficulty the lifeboat was manoeuvred to get alongside the *Acco* and the tow-rope re-attached. For another half hour the tow held and the *Acco* was slowly brought ever closer to Fleetwood. However, at the bottom end of Lune, around 1 mile southwest of Lune buoy, the seas became even higher and increasingly breaking. It seemed just a matter of time before the tow would part as 'twanging' pressure came on the tow-rope. The crew on the lifeboat saw a massive wave approaching the *Acco* and as if in slow motion the *Acco's* stern was lifted and the bow twisted off course, causing the *Acco* to surge forward with the force of the wave. As the same wave arrived at the lifeboat the stern rose and the combined movements of both vessels placed overwhelming tension on the tow that once again parted for a fourth time. This time the recoiling rope went under the stern as the lifeboat surfed forward when freed from the towing tension. As Roy brought the engine throttles back to stop the propellers, before they had stopped turning the tow-rope tangled in the starboard propeller. With only one engine available Roy could only use the port engine to keep steerage way on the lifeboat to keep clear of the *Acco* that yet again wallowed out of control as the seas struck her hull. Directly above the lifeboat propellers are removable inspection tubes that can be withdrawn vertically, specifically to enable direct access above the propeller and shaft in the event of them becoming fouled. Although this procedure is routinely practiced during exercises, usually in calm conditions, nothing prepares a crew for the reality of clearing a rope from the propeller in bad weather. Roy carefully used the port engine to turn the lifeboat bow on to the sea but he was concerned to stop the port engine as soon as possible to prevent the rope fouling both propellers.

The starboard inspection tube was withdrawn to expose the propeller beneath the hull so that the rope around the propeller could be cut free. Although this task was routinely practiced on exercises these were generally in relatively calm seas. Under the prevailing conditions on this day each time the stern lifted and then fell water was forced vertically up the tube, creating a fountain column of water that flooded the cockpit-well. A tool comprising a serrated edged knife affixed to a six foot pole was available specifically for the task of cutting any rope around the propeller but it became an arduous task to get knife at the end of the pole to engage and put sufficient pressure on the rope to saw through the thick strands. Water forcing up the vertical pipe hampered progress as Dave, Sandy and Norman each took a turn in attempting to clear the rope. It took a painstaking ten minutes before Norman felt the rope relax and become free as they pulled at it over the damaged stern rail.

Without using the port engine Roy gave the starboard engine a kick astern to try to clear the remains of the rope end. Fortunately, the fouled rope end came clear and pieces appeared on the surface at the starboard side of the lifeboats hull. Checking the port propeller was clear Roy engaged the port engine and as the propeller gripped the water the *Ann Letitia* responded to the rudder. Now with both engines available the lifeboat was brought around to re-approach the *Acco* that had drifted about a quarter of a mile apart from the lifeboat. It had been an uncomfortable time on the *Acco* because despite Noel's attempts to steer her to hold her head to sea, without her engine she continued to wallow almost broadside on. On board the *Acco* they had seen the difficulty the lifeboat was having with the rope in its propeller. Whilst they waited for the lifeboat to return Noel and the skipper went below to check on the passengers and explain what was happening. They also hoped they may be able to re-start the *Acco's* engine. As Noel and the skipper entered the main cabin all six people remained somnambulant but one by one Noel checked they were alright and explained to the adults what was happening.

Leaving the main cabin and entering the engine room there was an overpowering smell of fuel and Noel realised this must be fumes from fuel that must have leaked into the bilge. Although he was reluctant to attempt to restart the engine their situation was becoming desperate, with the lifeboat disabled, so he and the skipper tried to start the engine. Having completed the preparations, when they attempted to restart the engine although it turned the flywheel there was no sign of the engine firing and they abandoned further attempts. Because of the fuel in the bilge Noel decided to move the six people from the main cabin, to get them up into the fresher air in the wheelhouse. The six people were beyond protest and although it was a struggle to get them going they were all able to walk and climb the stairway to the wheelhouse. The wheelhouse was now crowded but Noel felt it was the safest place for them all and the fresh air did have a reviving effect.

After twenty five long minutes the lifeboat was seen to be underway and coming towards them, so Noel – this time accompanied by the skipper descended from the wheelhouse on to the deck. They both made their way for'ard to receive the tow rope once again. The tow rope had parted ahead of the tyre, so they both pulled the rope along with the tyre and the far end of the tow rope. As the lifeboat came close by the heaving line was passed across and caught on the *Acco* at the first attempt. The two ends of the tow rope were tied in a reef knot and additionally two half hitches were tied either side of the knot. Again the connected tow rope and tyre were passed over the bow of the *Acco* and the lifeboat kept sufficient engine revs to tension the rope and extend the tow to a satisfactory length. As the lifeboat took the strain the *Acco* started to move slowly forward through the water again, giving her steerage way that enabled the *Acco* to follow the lifeboat. For the first time in over an hour the incessant rolling reduced.

On board the lifeboat a tin of water from the emergency rations was opened to drink and a bar of chocolate was passed around the crew and for those who smoked a tin of cigarettes was opened. They weren't home yet but they knew they couldn't be that far from Lune buoy. It was now 09.45 and approximately two hours since the tow was commenced. Within minutes Lune buoy was sighted ahead of them, around 2 miles distant. A strong ebb tide was running out of

Morecambe Bay and with the 'wind over tide' effect the wave height was becoming amplified. Huge seas were building and anyone who is familiar with Morecambe Bay will appreciate that winds from a Northwesterly direction cause large seas to form and the combination of wind and tidal direction exaggerate the wave height.

Before the lifeboat and its tow had cleared Lune buoy the tow rope parted for a fifth time. Although there was a temptation for the coxswain to pluck the ten people off the *Acco* and abandon her, in the high seas that surrounded them in their current position again it was deemed to be too risky. For the fifth time the lifeboat was brought around to re-connect the tow and as the two craft rolled and pitched together what was left of the tow rope was prepared to be passed across. This time there was an additional problem, as the heaving line had not been thrown back across from the *Acco* on the previous occasion and with only two heaving lines originally on the lifeboat, both were now on the *Acco.* Rather than recover a line from the *Acco* coxswain Roy decided to approach close enough to pass the tow rope directly across to the Acco. Fenders were once again set on the port side and Roy slowly eased the lifeboat alongside the *Acco.* Timing was going to be critical as both vessels were pitching and rolling in the high seas surrounding them. With consummate skill the lifeboat inched in until less than six feet away when crewman Dave coiled three turns of towrope and threw it across to Noel who caught it first time and made it fast once again.

With little room for all ten people in the wheelhouse the tow continued up towards Danger Patch and King Scar buoy. There was a noticeable feeling of increasing relief as, ever so slowly, the seas started to moderate. The sandbanks behind King Scar were visible and it was about one hour before low water when the Acco passed abeam of King Scar buoy. The damaged mizzen mast of the lifeboat had been temporarily rigged to support the radio aerial wires and as the *Ann Letitia* passed King Scar buoy coxswain Roy told Brian, the mechanic, to radio the coastguard at Fleetwood and also contact Anglesey Radio to notify Liverpool coastguard of their position and estimated time of arrival at Fleetwood.

On board the *Acco,* spirits were rising as they could make out landmarks at Fleetwood. The seas were gradually subsiding as they slowly approached the Fleetwood Fairway buoy and the Wyre channel. As the lifeboat approached the Fairway Roy hand-signalled his intention to shorten the tow to make things more controllable for the transit up the channel towards Fleetwood. Without any need for adjustment on the *Acco* the lifeboat speed was reduced and two crew members adjusted the tow-rope on the towing bitts to reduce the length of the tow-rope. With the tow shortened the lifeboat throttles were increased and the pair of vessels passed Fairway buoy, entering the Fleetwood channel just half an hour before low water. Even though the wind was still at gale force the shelter afforded by the sandbanks of the North Wharf gave shelter and the passage was relatively calm. Spirits were returning to normal by this time and some of the occupants of the wheelhouse departed to get some fresh air on the open deck.

Returning to station with *Acco* in tow
photo Ian Atkinson

Noel again went to get his pipe from his pocket but had second thoughts when he remembered the fuel that had spilled into the bilges. On the lifeboat spirits were also up as they entered the Fleetwood channel and for the first time this trip Norman Pendlebury cracked a joke, suddenly breaking the tension of the past six hours and giving a laugh to all on-board. Soon after 11.00 a.m. the lifeboat and its tow passed the open doors of the lifeboat-house where preparations had been made for re-housing the lifeboat.

The *Acco* was towed to the North End quay, where it was eased alongside the wooden structure and using its own mooring ropes was tied to the jetty. An overwhelming feeling of relief came over all the lifeboat crew as they realized what they had achieved in rescuing the nine people from the *Acco* and saving the vessel itself. They suddenly felt shivers of cold as for the first time in the past hours they realised just how wet they all were beneath their outer oilskin clothing.

When the *Ann Letitia Russell* lifeboat was re-housing on the slipway the damage done by the rope parting and re-coiling against the stanchions and safety chains on the stern rail could be seen, as the stern rails on the port side were completely missing.

Re-housing *Ann Letitia Russell* after *Acco* incident.
Note damaged stern-rails. photo Ian Atkinson

Interview with former crewman Norman Pendlebury

Norman Pendlebury was running a plumbing and heating business when he began to help out at the lifeboat station where a family friend was a crew member.

The old order of all volunteers being local fishermen was changing as men from other walks of life were drawn into the service.

Norman - who was always ready with a joke, which eased many a tough situation, recalls "It was early on a Sunday morning when we went for the *Acco* and the weather was bad right from the off. We went along through The Neckings (a channel close inshore to the coast but only available at certain states of the tide) until we reached Rossall Point.

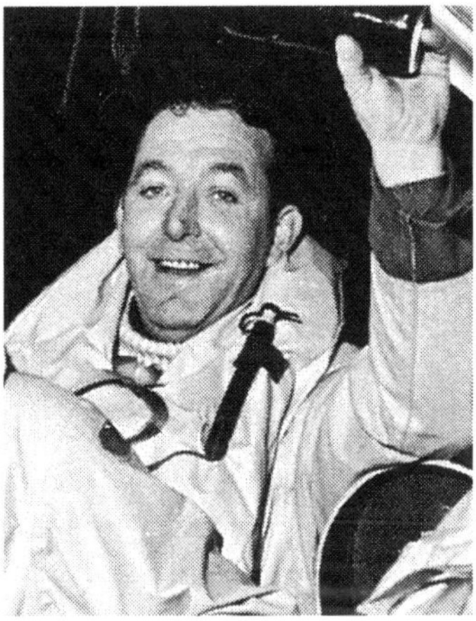

Norman Pendlebury

"I was not surprised to hear that the Coastguard reported us jumping out of the water. She was like a rocking horse". It was particularly rough at the western end of The Neckings. It was the sort of day when you think: "What am I doing here? I should be at home in bed!"

"Mind you, I don't know why people did lifeboats at all in those days. There was no shelter. It was crazy."

From Rossall Point, the lifeboat began a 15 mile journey to the Morecambe Bay Lightvessel. It took more than two hours.

"She was taking so much punishment. It was as bad if not worse than I ever experienced in my 10 years as a crew member. We had some bad weather services over the years but I think the *Acco* was the worst."

Said Norman: " Roy Mitchinson was a good coxswain. He could give orders and command his crew which a Coxswain has to do. As for Noel, I always felt very confident about him. He was very capable and calm."

The seas were so big that as the lifeboat sank into a trough the mast of the *Acco* behind them could not be seen above the crest of the following seas. Sometimes waves broke onboard the lifeboat.

" I was hit in the back by a big lump of water which is like being hit by a bag of cement – water is heavy stuff. We were all soaked to the skin".

" In the end we got back to Fleetwood and moored them up at the old North End Quay".

"Noel should have got a medal for what he did that day – maybe we all should. We never thought about recognition at the time – we never expected anything. But, years after, you think back and think there should have been recognition for a service like that".

"At the time we were just glad to be back home in Fleetwood and glad to have got the people back safely. You got a sense of achievement and that was it."

Despite an ordeal of nearly 10 hours, the crew had not finished their duties. Once they got the *Ann Letitia Russell* back up the slipway and into the boathouse – which was not an easy task – she had to be washed down with fresh water and made ready for the next service . It might come in an hour, a day, a week, a month.......

Norman recalls the strong comradeship of the Fleetwood lifeboat team in those days.

" The public bar at the North Euston Hotel was our office and that's where we went that Sunday afternoon for a pint or two before went home for some dry clothes. That's how it was in those days and I look back on those 10 years as a good time in my life".

"Every time we went out it was like an adventure. I would not have missed it for the world."

The pre-VHF radio-communications era

Even in the mid-1970's it was the exception rather than the norm for vessels to have reliable radio-communications. Before the availability of relatively low-cost VHF transceivers, with modest aerial requirements, the communications with fishing vessels were generally on the 'Trawler Band' around 1.90 MHz. In the age of 'valve' radios this equipment could be unreliable and prone to breakdown. Without dependable communications the lifeboat was often launched to search for vessels that were overdue and reported missing. All-night searches were common due to lack of communication with a vessel that may have broken down. It was only when the lifeboat *Lady of Lancashire* was fitted with a VHF radio direction finder in 1978 that bearings could be taken of a transmission received, that could be used to locate the position of the sending station, which may itself have been uncertain of its position.

Ann Letitia Russell lifeboat towing Prawner *Lassie*. 28th July, 1974

The above photograph shows the inshore fishing vessel *Lassie (FD293)* as she is being towed past the lifeboat station into the Jubilee Quay on 28th July, 1974, having earlier broken down with engine problems off Blackpool and signalled for assistance.

The Watson Class non-self-righting lifeboat *Ann Letitia Russell* remained on station until 1976 when she was replaced by the Waveney Class lifeboat *Lady of Lancashire*.

This was the end of the era of slipway launches and in preparation for the new lifeboat that had to remain permanently afloat a special dock was constructed with a pontoon for the lifeboat to tie up to.

Since the early days of the lifeboat station at Fleetwood the lifeboats had been slipway launched. The first boathouse with a slipway was built in 1879; before that the lifeboat had been housed on a horse drawn trailer in a boathouse on the Promenade (1859-1863) and a brick-built boathouse off Pharos Square (1863-1879).

Lifeboat *Ann Letitia Russell* returning from exercise. 1975
photograph courtesy John Dales

Following the retirement of the *Ann Letitia Russell* lifeboat she was sailed from Fleetwood to Beaumaris and after a short period in the reserve fleet was eventually sold from the R.N.L.I.

(In 2015 a preservation group was formed to return the former *Ann Letitia Russell* lifeboat hull to Fleetwood with a view to restorating her to her former condition).

Fleetwood Lifeboat *Ann Letitia Russell* on slipway photo John Dales

The days of slipway launching at Fleetwood were over, as the Waveney class lifeboat with its exposed propellers needed to lie afloat all the time.

It was a sad site to see the demolition of the wooden former lifeboat-house in 1977.

Demolishing the Boathouse in 1977 photograph John Dales

The lifeboat-house had been at this place, East of the Lower Lighthouse since 1901 and the same boathouse had been originally built a similar distance West of the Lower lighthouse in 1892 but due to siltation causing difficulties in launching it was re-located to this final position. It is understood that the move was achieved with 'jacks' and rollers.

Fleetwood Lifeboat crew December 1984 picture Evening Gazette

Rear row Left to right: Shore helper John Birkbeck, William Rawcliffe (jnr), Deputy Coxswain Stephen Musgrave, Coxswain Ian Fairclough, Mechanic Andrew Griffin, Tim Merrill, Dave Bolland, Shore helper John Duckworth.

Front row Left to right: Dave Owen, Adrian Whittaker, William 'Bill' Rawcliffe and Barrie Farmer.

The former lifeboat house was replaced by a wooden assembly hut. This picture shows the lifeboat crew and shore-helpers in the days of the Lady of Lancashire lifeboat in the 1980's.

Preparing to re-house *Ann Letitia Russell* photograph Ian Atkinson

Ann Letitia Russell keel on the slipway photograph Ian Atkinson

6 LIFEBOAT *'LADY OF LANCASHIRE'* (1976 - 1989)

The former Watson class lifeboat *Ann Letitia Russell* was replaced by a faster offshore lifeboat. Based on an American Coastguard Cutter design this Waveney class lifeboat had an operational speed of 16 knots. The Duke of Kent named the lifeboat *Lady of Lancashire* at a service of dedication on 20th July, 1976. She had been provided by the gift of an anonymous donor, who in later years was named as Mr. Philip Leigh-Bramwell, a Lancashire businessman. Because this lifeboat had exposed propellers it could not be slipway launched. A special lifeboat dock was built, in the present location of the lifeboat station, adjacent to the Knott-End Ferry dock.

Waveney class lifeboat *Lady of Lancashire* Artist Ken Frost

Her faster speed (almost double that if her predecessor) was extremely useful but this was achieved by having her propellers exposed beneath the hull, unlike the *Ann Letitia Russell* where the propellers were protected in tunnels.

David Scott coxswain 1976 - 1980

Roy Mitchinson was succeeded by David Scott who was the first Coxswain of the *Lady of Lancashire*. He served for four years.

Lifeboat Coxswain Dave Scott

David Scott was one of 13 children. His father, Charles, was skipper and owner of the inshore trawler *Onward Fisher,* which made history as the first stern-fishing craft in Fleetwood. David, his older brother Walter and younger brother Peter all sailed with their father. Peter later became Station Mechanic at Fleetwood.

The Scott family boat was a successful craft.

The *'Lady'* was soon in action under David's command.

A notable service came when the angling boat *Wahine* ran aground about four miles from Fleetwood. Four of the eight men onboard decided to wade ashore over the sands and raise the alarm.

Later, in rough seas and very heavy rain, David used radar to locate the *Wahine* which had refloated on the rising tide. The engine would not start so the lifeboat began to tow the craft back to Fleetwood. However, the *Wahine* was taking in water faster than the crew could bail it out. In very difficult conditions the lifeboat crew took the four men off the sinking craft. Two were injured and needed hospital treatment.

An unusual service came early one morning when a December gale was blowing but it took only eight minutes for a full crew to arrive at the boathouse.

The Fleetwood trawler *Gavina* was towing an Icelandic trawler into port and the lifeboatmen sprayed oil on the water's surface to help operations as the tow line broke twice and had to be reconnected. The Icelandic ship had lost her steering and the lifeboat used another tow line to help guide her round in a sharp turn to enter the Wyre channel and successfully enter the port.

When the *Lady of Lancashire* arrived, a new Second Coxswain was needed and the Station's Honorary Secretary, Dick Willoughby, came up with a solution. Former top trawler skipper Bill Rawcliffe was now working ashore as manager of the Boston Deep Sea Fishing Company and had become Dick's deputy launching authority at the lifeboat station. He had passed his colour blindness test as a young fisherman. He qualified as a skipper at the age of 21 - the minimum time possible after becoming a trawlerman at the age of 15. So Bill donned a lifejacket and later had the distinction of commanding the *Ann Letitia Russell* on her final voyage from Fleetwood when she was retired and sailed to the boatyard in Beaumaris, North Wales.

Fleetwood Lifeboat Crew photograph on *Lady of Lancashire* in 1976 preparing for the Service of Dedication.
Rear Row: David Owen Stephen Musgrave, Adrian Whittaker, Mechanic Andrew Griffin , Frank Whitehead. Front Row: Barrie Farmer, Peter Gow John Howard, Coxswain David Scott, Second Coxswain Bill Rawcliffe. Sitting: Ian Atkinson, John Duckworth.

Ian Fairclough coxswain 1980 -1994

Ian Fairclough was only a schoolboy when he first got a taste of the sea hanging out among the yachtsmen of Skippool Creek up the River Wyre from his home town of Fleetwood.

He decided on a maritime career as an apprentice deck officer in the merchant navy after a stint at the training establishment Indefatigable in North Wales. Later, Ian sampled life in the emergency services when he became a firefighter with the Blackpool brigade for three years. Then he went afloat again when he joined the ranks of Fleetwood's inshore fishermen down at the Jubilee Quay.

" I was always interested in fishing and I bought a boat called *Fruitful* from Peterhead and sailed her down to Fleetwood.

Lifeboat Coxswain Ian Fairclough

Ian's new career was the start of a long learning curve but it was successful and he progressed to bigger and better boats. Much of the seabed in Morecambe Bay is composed of sand and mud but Ian proved that a living could be made by setting pots on the stony areas – 'the roughs' in Jubilee Quay speak – to catch crabs and lobsters. Two of his boats, *Pilgrim* and *Hannibal*, were built for him as brand new craft.

In the Seventies, *Pilgrim* was one of a group of Fleetwood boats sold to African owners and that took Ian to that continent on a trip that found him and his colleagues being arrested as Russian spies and thrown into jail! Guards would often push their AK47 assault rifles in through the window. Would they squeeze the trigger?

" We were very glad when the door opened two days later and we were flown home!"

He returned to the Jubilee Quay world and was appointed Coxswain in 1980 not long after joining the lifeboat crew.

" I had been on the fringe for a few years – it's something you seem to drift into."

Coxswains must have the backing of their crew in order to be appointed and Ian proved himself to be an able man at the helm of the *Lady of Lancashire*, which was of the Waveney class based on an American Coastguard design, known affectionately as a Spam Can.

"I had an affinity with that boat – she was a wonderful tool for the job."

One of the worst days for the *'Lady'* and her crew was in 1983 when a man drowned as he tried to rescue a pet dog and three police officers drowned as they tried to rescue him just off Blackpool promenade in The Gynn area. " We took a very big sea off Rossall Point on the way down to Blackpool," said Ian. " The world went green!" They searched very close in off the North Shore promenade when the lifeboat might easily have been overturned or dashed into the concrete sea defences in the 20 foot waves and heavy, breaking swells. He was forced to sail broadside on to the incoming seas as he crept forward through the search area. Then, when a particularly big wave came rolling out of the west the trick was to swing the *'Lady'* sharply round to take that sea bow on. The hull design and engine power were vital to the success of a manoeuvre like that but the risks were high.

" We were glad to get back to Fleetwood that day," Ian admitted.

All the more so because he had decided to take an extra risk. An R.N.L.I. mechanic had been working on the engines of the *Lady of Lancashire* when the call came and he had removed equipment designed to help in a capsize situation. There was no time to replace it and Ian decided, in view of the gravity of the situation at Blackpool, to go without it.

Like all experienced seafarers Ian has known frightening times when it looked as though the sea could win.

"A Coxswain must not show his crew what he might be feeling on a bad day. You respond to a call and concentrate completely on the job in hand. Sometimes you feel apprehensive – but you get on with the job and keep your feelings to yourself."

Helicopters play a vital part in the rescue at sea scenario but when the weather goes against them – wind, fog, snow - then the lifeboats come into their own.

Apart from his duties at Fleetwood, Ian worked for the R.N.L.I. nationally with Staff Coxswain Brian Gerrard who had been the Fleetwood Station Mechanic. Working out of R.N.L.I. headquarters in Poole they moved lifeboats around the coast of Britain and there are few lifeboat stations Ian has not visited. They took new boats on trial runs and were involved in testing new designs.

Ian reflects: "Basically, I like driving boats. It was a great privilege and an honour to be able to do what I have done in my time with the R.N.L.I."

He served 17 years as Coxswain at Fleetwood and was recognised for some of the outstanding services he led.

Ian had been very happy to command the *Lady of Lancashire* but he knew that the Tyne-class lifeboats – like the *William Street* – were a much safer platform for lifeboat-men to work from. Among other things they offered much better shelter to the crew on passage to and from a casualty.

His wife Sandra was closely involved with the fund-raising activities at Fleetwood for many years as part of a close-knit group of supporters at the station.

Nowadays, Ian and Sandra sail the calmer waters of the canal system together in their narrow boat *Alexandrian.*

September 14th, 1987 Fishing Vessel *Galilean*

On September 14th, 1987, the inshore fishing vessel *Galilean* had spent the day trawling south of Blackpool. Fishing had been good but around tea-time and before the skipper was ready to return to Fleetwood the weather deteriorated, with increasingly strong South Westerly winds. He then noticed an unusual noise and discovered water in the engine room. A preliminary search was undertaken but they were unable to see where the leak was coming from so they hauled the trawl and started to head back to Fleetwood. With their pump running to keep the water level down they checked the boat from stem to stern. The water wasn't just in the engine room, it was also in the fish-room and forepeak. Eventually they moved some gear and located the leak around the waterline, between two planks. Despite their efforts to prevent water entering the hull it was slowly becoming a losing battle and their concern was increasing. For almost an hour the engine kept going but whilst still off the Blackpool coast, West of Blackpool Tower, at around 8.30 p.m. the water level had reached a point where the engine spluttered and stopped. Without the engine power the pump ceased to function, with nothing then to prevent the water level rising as water continued to seep through the hole.

The skipper made a distress call on the VHF radio, stating they were taking water and the engine now stopped. They were disabled around 5 miles West of Blackpool Tower, with two persons on board, requesting immediate assistance. Coastguard officers received the message and contacted Fleetwood Lifeboat officials advising immediate launch of the offshore lifeboat. A relief Waveney class lifeboat, *Arthur and Blanche Harris* was on temporary service at Fleetwood. Within ten minutes the lifeboat crew were geared up, on-board and moorings were slipped. Around 20.40 hrs the lifeboat proceeded to sea and it was already on the edge of darkness. As they left communications were established with Liverpool Coastguard who confirmed the position of the casualty and the number of person on-board. The winds were already strong from a West South Westerly direction. As the lifeboat turned Southwards between King Scar and Shell Wharf buoy the seas were rolling the lifeboat such that speed had to be reduced. The *Arthur and Blanche Harris* (44-006) relief lifeboat was an earlier build than the station boat *Lady of Lancashire (44-015)* and not fitted with a VHF radio direction finder, so although radio contact was made with *Galilean* it was not possible to get a relative bearing to indicate and confirm her position. Approaching the reported position in darkness a white illuminating flare was fired. As the parachute drifted downwind towards the shore the *Galilean* was spotted just over a mile away. When the lifeboat approached another flare was sent up. It burst into the night sky and the *Galilean* could be clearly seen ahead of the lifeboat. She was down by the stern, wallowing and rolling heavily in the breaking seas. With her stern low in the water the nets and ropes on the aft deck were already beginning to float free, trailing over the side. This gave concern on the lifeboat about hazards that could foul the propellers if the lifeboat approached too close. Coxswain Ian Fairclough manoeuvred the lifeboat to position it ahead of the *Galilean's* bow, approaching from downwind with the lifeboat's bow head to wind, hopefully away from any obstruction. The lifeboat was brought slowly forward to cross *Galilean's* bow at a safe distance but close enough to throw a heaving line across, albeit with difficulty in the strong winds, with a tow rope attached. The first and second attempts failed as the heaving line missed the bow. It was then necessary to take the lifeboat around again to re-position it off the bow. The next attempt also fell short and only at a fourth attempt was the crewman on the bow of *Galilean* able to catch the heaving line and pull the tow rope across, securing it on their bow fitting.

It was almost two hours after the lifeboat launched, around 10.20 p.m. when the tow was commenced. Only slow progress could be made at less than 4 knots as the *Galilean* was slowly filling with water, making her increasingly heavy to tow. The stern was becoming noticeably deeper in the water as time went on but the tow continued in a North Easterly direction for over an hour. The lifeboats searchlight was trained on the *Galilean* to keep her under observation. Shortly after midnight the skipper appeared on deck waving his arms to attract attention. The lifeboat coxswain slowed the engines in response to reduce speed. As the tow rope slackened it was pulled back onto the lifeboat. The skipper shouted across that things were bad; the water level was rising quickly and the *Galilean* was starting to sink. Suddenly a heavy sea struck the hull, rolling her over to starboard and carrying away part of her bulwark. The debris of nets, ropes and other gear trailing over the side of the *Galilean* was increasingly hazardous, so by agreement the skipper and crewman inflated their life-raft in preparation to abandon their vessel. The *Galilean* had rolled back upright, then listed onto its port side. Accepting the inevitable fact that the *Galilean* would soon sink beneath the waves the coxswain gave the order to chop the tow rope that still connected the lifeboat to the *Galilean.* With the tow disconnected the lifeboat was re-positioned to stand off down wind (of the fishing boat's hull), in readiness for the crew to take to their life-raft and float across to the lifeboat. To illuminate the area a parachute flare was put up. The life-raft was seen to inflate and the two crew members stepped into it. By now the *Galilean's* stern was beneath the surface and the bow was noticeably lower in the water. The *Galilean* became awash from stem to stern, with seas rolling right across the main-deck as the crew let go the painter, releasing the life-raft to drift away downwind to the lifeboat. The distance was short, only about 50 metres away, as the life-raft was wind-blown across the narrow gap. Under the illumination of another parachute flare the situation had rapidly worsened for the *Galilean* as she was sinking fast. It wasn't sudden and the glow from the illuminating flare gave an eeriness to the events that seemed to be happening in slow motion before our eyes. The two crew arrived alongside the lifeboat and both crew members were speedily transferred to the lifeboat.

The lifeboat remained on scene, taking time to confirm the precise coordinates of the position where the *Galilean* had sunk, so the Coastguards and relevant authorities could be notified. This position was radioed to the Liverpool Coastguard. The depth was reasonably shallow and when the hull settled on the sea-bed the top of the main and mizzen masts were still visible above the surface. Fish boxes, plastic floats, ropes, nets, an empty gas bottle and other items littered the sea around the wrecked hull and an oily slick began to spread across the surface.

The two crew from the *Galilean* had remained reasonably dry but were shocked by their experience, having witnessed their vessel sinking beneath them. As the lifeboat left the scene they looked back at the empty sea until the mast heads disappeared into the darkness. They then went below into the main cabin to get warm. The lifeboat returned to station at full speed, arriving back at Fleetwood at 01.10 a.m.

For his skill, courage and determination during this service, Coxswain Ian Fairclough was awarded the 'Thanks on Vellum' by the R.N.L.I., with Vellum Service Certificates being presented to each of the other members of the crew.

Lifeboat *Lady of Lancashire 44-015* photo John Dales

Lady of Lancashire in lifeboat pen photo John Dales

7 LIFEBOAT '*WILLIAM STREET*' (1989 - 2016)

In October 1989 a new Tyne class lifeboat replaced the Waveney class *Lady of Lancashire*. At 47 feet long she was three foot longer than her predecessor and faster, with an operational speed of 19 knots. Built at the FBM yard in Cowes, Isle of Wight, for the first time the crew were protected from the elements in an enclosed cabin.

There were two steering positions; one in the main cabin and an outside one behind the aft end of the main cabin, towards the stern. This lifeboat was funded from the W.O. Street Foundation, together with money gifted from Miss Hilda Richmond and legacies from Mr Francis Balshaw and Major Percy Holley. William Street had been a well known Lancashire businessman. A naming and dedication ceremony took place in Fleetwood Marina in May 1990.

Tyne class lifeboat *William Street* Artist Ken Frost

Chris Hurst M.B.E. coxswain 1994 - 2007

When he moved to the seaside from Birmingham as a 12-year-old schoolboy Chris Hurst couldn't believe his luck. He immediately loved the beach and the sea in his new home town of Fleetwood and quickly discovered the world of inshore fishing boats through school friends. "My first trip to sea was on the Scott family boat *Onward Fisher* trying to tow a stranded trawler called *Hamoaze* off Pilling Sands. I was 12 at the time and spent most of the time in the cabin looking into a bucket. But when Skipper Charlie Scott asked if I would like to come again I said yes and that was it."

Chris was not a keen scholar but when he decided on a course at the Fleetwood Nautical Campus to join the merchant navy as an apprentice deck officer he worked hard for a change and managed to pass the required GCSE grades. " I went to sea for four years and was planning on taking my Second Mates certificate when I met a girl called Anne and decided I did not want to spend the majority of my time on a ship." The couple married and Chris began a new, and successful, career in the brewing industry. " But if you have an allegiance to the sea you want to get involved with it."

The answer was a weekend enterprise in which Chris operated a charter boat taking fishing parties out into Morecambe Bay. The local knowledge he built up through this work and the expertise he had already gained at sea and at college made him an ideal candidate as an R.N.L.I. crewman.

He followed his friend Stephen Musgrave as Second Coxswain.

"Ian Fairclough was the Coxswain then and he was an excellent seaman. I learned a great deal from him."

Like many other lifeboat-men over the years, Chris remembers that some of the worst conditions he experienced at sea did not result in memorable rescues or historic services.

" When we had to go searching for people close inshore at Blackpool it could get pretty hairy. We would be broadside on in heavy weather and sometimes it seemed an eternity as the boat came round to go head to the weather which was a safer position."

Lifeboat Coxswain Chris Hurst MBE

One epic trip was to a gas carrier called *Chartsman* which had broken down off Barrow and was dragging her anchors.

" It was a good Force 11 and we stood by until she got going again".

On the next visit to the port of Barrow the port pilot was Peter Woodworth, Fleetwood LOM. After introducing himself to the Master he said that he had to call out the lifeboat on his previous visit, to which the master replied 'Ah yes, there I was, two anchors down, main engine would not start and I'm dragging backwards into shallower and shallower water. What I really wanted was a dirty great tug and all I got was a f****** lifeboat!!'

Peter could not think of any suitable reply to this all he remembers is saying 'Ah,......... yes.'

After Coxswain Fairclough retired in 1997, Chris took over the command with his old schoolmate Peter Scott, the Station Mechanic, now taking the rank of Second Coxswain/Mechanic.

Chris retired in 2007 after 23 years service at sea with the R.N.L.I. during which time his skill and leadership was officially acknowledged several times.

" In my time I saw the balance of services move away from a majority of fishing boats and working craft to a majority of leisure craft. Many services may appear routine but you have to remember that, to the people you are helping, that service is a top service."

Subsequently, Chris was awarded an MBE for his services to sea safety. Prince Charles told him: "We, as a family, hold the R.N.L.I. in very high regard."

Chris has continued his work with the R.N.L.I. as a Deputy Launching Authority at Fleetwood Station.

12th December, 1998 *Pendle Witch*

On Saturday evening 12th December, 1998, an ex-naval pinnace named *Pendle Witch* got into difficulty when its engine failed off Fleetwood. The *Pendle Witch* had sailed from Skippool Creek earlier that day with three people on board. They had been out on an angling trip for 12 hours and the weather had been reasonable during the day. When the engine failed, despite repeated attempts they were unable to start the engine and drained the battery, preventing the VHF radio from functioning so they were unable to communicate on the distress channel. The weather had been deteriorating overnight and those on board were concerned that the wind was strengthening all the time. As the 11 metre motor launch had broken down within sight of Wyre Light at around 3.30 a.m. they knew where they were but in the North Westerly near gale force conditions even though they streamed all their anchor rope it failed to grab the seabed on Lighthouse Bank and they were drifting eastwards towards Bernard Wharf. Once again they attempted to use the VHF radio but having flattened the battery there was no sign of life. The three men realised the difficulty they were in, so in desperation the skipper tried using his mobile phone to make a 999 call to the Coastguard to request assistance. Liverpool Coastguard received the call via the telephone network and contacted Fleetwood Lifeboat Operations Manager (LOM) Captain Peter Woodworth, explaining the situation and advising him to launch the All Weather Lifeboat *William Street.* The message was immediately conveyed to coxswain Chris Hurst who summoned his crew. Whilst driving his car down to the lifeboat station along the promenade he caught sight of a red parachute distress signal in the vicinity of Wyre Light, so he knew the urgency of the situation. It was a cold December morning with the ground wet from overnight rain. When the lifeboat left the pen a rain shower had reduced the visibility so it was difficult to see beyond the Knott Spit buoy. The wind had seemed to be around force 5 from the North West but before they were 300 yards from the 'pen' they felt the full strength of the wind and it was around gale force.

Progress down the channel to Wyre Light was uneventful, apart from the worsening weather conditions. The *Pendle Witch* had been reported to be in the vicinity of Fleetwood Fairway buoy, however on arrival there was no sighting of the vessel, yet Chris knew he had seen a distress rocket himself. Coxswain Chris Hurst ordered a crew member to fire one white parachute illuminating flare, aiming it upwind of the lifeboat. Within seconds the rocket climbed into the sky, rising to around 500 feet with the inclined trajectory in the strong wind. At first nothing was sighted but as the strong wind carried the burning flare past the lifeboat a crew member spotted the casualty in the surf on the eastern bank of the river. It was getting towards low water and Coxswain Chris understood the dilemma that faced him only too well. Four choices were considered:

- Standing off and attempting to fire a rocket line across.
- Go into the shallows and risk the lifeboat and the lives of those on board.
- Call for backup with the Inshore Lifeboat (ILB), or
- Request helicopter assistance.

Considering these options he quickly rationalised that the helicopter was more than 40 minutes away and that would be too late for those on board the *Pendle Witch*. The ILB backup was rejected because the weather on scene was beyond the safe working limits for this craft. Although there was an option to try a rocket line, in the shoal conditions the distance was too great. It therefore became 'Hobsons Choice' for Coxswain Chris if he was going to stand any chance of rescuing the persons on board the pinnace. Just as he had made his mind up to take the lifeboat into the shallow waters the *Pendle Witch* was perilously grounding in - the pinnace suddenly turned onto its beam ends. Chris knew that time was short to do anything to save the lives of those on-board the *Pendle Witch.* Knowing the area he could see that the craft was in great danger of breaking up on the mussel-bed banks of Barnet Bank. Through his local knowledge as a former angling charter boat skipper he knew that if he took the lifeboat back out into deeper water he could go north about around the top of Barnet Bank and come in to approach the pinnace around the back side of the bank. The *Pendle Witch* was being driven wave by wave eastwards over the top of Barnet Bank, pounding her mercilessly as each wave lifted the hull and dropped it down heavily on the sea-bed, causing timber crunching shudders to reverberate throughout the hull. For those on board the *Pendle Witch* they felt it was only a matter of time before the hull would succumb to the relentless pounding it was taking. Having seen the lifeboat approach the three people on board the pinnace saw the lifeboat disappear into the darkness of the night. Anxious moments passed and the pounding continued relentlessly before the lifeboat re-appeared from a different direction and closed upon them. Suddenly the lifeboat's hull was looming over them in the same surf line that had been their torment for almost an hour. The searchlight beam swung round to illuminate them and the lifeboat crewman on the bow showed a heaving line and tow-rope that signaled their intention to pass it across. From the deck of the lifeboat they saw the skipper of the *Pendle Witch* crawl on his hands and knees onto the foredeck to ready himself to catch the heaving line.

On the *Pendle Witch* they could hear the lifeboat's hull repeatedly bumping on the bank as it came closer and closer in the shallow water, with each wave lifting it forwards. Without further signals the heaving line was airborne as it was thrown across from the lifeboat. It landed on board the pinnace roughly mid-ships and the crewman scrambled forward to retrieve it, understanding that he needed to get it to the foredeck for the skipper to fasten it to the bow fitting. The pinnace was still rolling violently with each breaking wave that struck them. It was a struggle for the skipper to get the line to the foredeck yet he summoned all his strength to both cling on to their vessel and work the line round to the bow fitting. The lifeboat towrope had been laid up the port side deck from the towing bollard and rope drum towards the stern. As the pinnace skipper struggled to pull the tow rope across it became heavier as the length in the water increased and he doubted he had the strength to finish the task, yet he summoned every ounce of energy knowing that their lives literally depended upon his effort. Fate dealt another blow when the end of the towrope came onto the pinnace's deck he found that the diameter of the towrope was too large to secure to their foredeck fitting. He was an experienced seaman who knew he had to sort something out and he looped the heaving line several times around the foredeck cleat and tied the loops repeatedly to the towrope; several thicknesses of heaving line thereby increasing the overall breaking strain. Under the searchlight's illumination the bowman had seen the problem on the foredeck and communicated this to the coxswain. He could also see what the skipper was trying to do. The lifeboat was barely a boats length away when the skipper indicated that the towrope was connected. Coxswain Chris Hurst knew that there was now a weak link in this connection and he couldn't apply full power to reverse out of the situation. He told the bowman to make fast the lifeboat towrope on the bow fitting of the lifeboat. A message was shouted across to the pinnace telling the skipper to either get the anchor back on board or chop the anchor rope. When the towrope was secure as each wave lifted the pinnace Chris applied reverse power on the engines to get the pinnace and the lifeboat away into deeper water. At first nothing seemed to happen and *Pendle Witch* stubbornly rolled in the breakers without shifting. Wave by wave the lifeboat tried to shift the pinnace's hull but it was fast aground on the bank. The lifeboat was repeatedly touching the bottom with resounding thumps and Chris knew he was going to have to be bold if he was going to get out of this situation. He saw a larger wave approaching and seeing this wash right over the pinnace he took the opportunity to apply more power, giving full astern thrust. The pinnace moved and to everyone's relief its hull started to bounce on the seabed as the lifeboat and their tow moved together into slightly deeper water. Both vessels were still in the broken water of the surf-line so it was not yet possible to take the three crew off the pinnace onto the lifeboat. However, the pinnace was freed from the grips of Barnet Bank. Waves were still breaking clean across the deck of the pinnace and with the lifeboat stern first onto the seas each wave was slamming the stern and breaking across the aft cabin to land in the well deck, draining away through the scuppers.

Time had been against them but against the odds they had extricated *Pendle Witch* from immediate danger. It would have been only a few more minutes before the hull would have succumbed to the extreme forces as it was dropped wave upon wave on the hard stony ground of the mussel beds. Now they had an opportunity to pluck the three men to safety but they weren't out of immediate danger yet. The depth sounder started to show a reading as they slowly edged away from the aerated water in the surf and with solid water beneath the lifeboats hull the depth started to register again on the echo-sounder. With ten feet of water beneath them they knew they were winning as the lifeboat continued to move astern with the pinnace tethered to the lifeboats bow. Although tantalisingly close to safety Coxswain Chris wanted to be well clear of the uneven bottom and into deeper water before he turned the lifeboat around. Wave upon wave crashed against the stern of the lifeboat dropping solid water back as far as the steering position, soaking all those on the exposed deck. Before the depth sounder reached twenty feet of water beneath the lifeboats hull Coxswain Chris gauged that he could now sort out the tow. Briefing his crew he prepared them to release the tow from the lifeboats bow, keeping the slackening tow rope under control as he reduced stern speed, enabling the lifeboat to be turned into the wind and sea thereby resuming the tow to the stern of the lifeboat. Using the lifeboat engines he slowly turned the lifeboat around, retrieving the tow rope slack and paying it out again as the *Pendle Witch* dropped astern of the lifeboat. With the three persons still on the pinnace Chris put both engines ahead to get the lifeboat into deeper water and out of the breaking waves.

Within a few hundred metres their situation improved, with the seas becoming noticeably less breaking. Both engines were stopped and the crew put fenders out on the port side ready to bring the pinnace alongside. The searchlight was trained aft as the gap between the lifeboat and *Pendle Witch* reduced to less than a boats length. Using the lifeboat engines Coxswain Chris ensured the pinnace would come slowly alongside as the tow-rope was retrieved onto its storage drum.

As soon as the hull was alongside the three people were brought across onto the lifeboat. It had taken twenty minutes to drag the pinnace from the bank and into sufficient water to rescue the three people but they were now on-board the lifeboat and safely in the for'ard cabin. The skipper explained that they had been out from Skippool on a day fishing trip. Engine trouble had prevented them getting back twelve hours later as planned. The weather had deteriorated and despite best efforts they had been unable to re-start the engine, flattening the batteries in the process. Knowing their anchor wasn't holding and seeing their drift towards the banks they had sent up distress rockets to indicate their difficulties.

The pinnace was slowly towed back to Fleetwood and tied alongside the North End berth, waiting for the tide to get her back up to Skippool.

Recognition for this outstanding service came as a Letter of Thanks from the R.N.L.I. Director Andrew Freemantle MBE and a Letter of Appreciation from Mike Vlasto, the R.N.L.I's Chief of Operations at that time, praising the excellent teamwork in rescuing the three people from the *Pendle Witch* under arduous conditions.

Paul Ashworth coxswain 2007 - 2013

The thrills and spills of windsurfing were Paul Ashworth's introduction to the world of the sea.

Lifeboat Coxswain Paul Ashworth

The sport was his relaxation from running the family heating and plumbing business but he saw a business opportunity linked to his hobby. Paul developed a separate business selling sails, boards and other equipment and teaching people how to use them. He had a shop in Fleetwood and became a tenant of Wyre Council using the Marine Boating Lake for his board sailing school and, later, another building on the seafront Lower Promenade.

During this time he moved from his native Thornton to live in Fleetwood and found himself next door neighbour to Captain David Eccles who commanded ro-ro ships for the Pandoro company carrying truckloads of goods across the Irish Sea between Fleetwood and Larne. He was also part of the Fleetwood R.N.L.I. operation and suggested to Paul that he might like to sample the lifeboat world himself. "I thought lifeboatmen were all fishermen –I knew nothing about it. But I went to sea on a training trip that first night and it was a thrill. I enjoyed it."

Paul began to serve an apprenticeship as was the custom in the days when R.N.L.I. crew training was much less formal. "I knew nothing about it – I got in the way of people who did. I spent a lot of time on shore handling the mooring ropes." Gradually, Paul's perseverance in turning out for emergencies and learning more about his duties was rewarded by Coxswain Chris Hurst who began to include him in his crew on active services so that he developed into a competent, fully-fledged lifeboat-man.

Paul successfully completed a Royal Yachting Association Yachtmaster Certificate demonstrating the theoretical, navigational and practical skills he had learned and did some training at R.N.L.I. HQ in Poole.

He was chosen as Second Coxswain and gained experience of command on a variety of services before Coxswain Chris Hurst retired because of the R.N.L.I. maximum age rules and Paul took over at Christmas, 2007. The ever-changing world of the R.N.L.I. had seen women taking an equal part with men as lifeboat crew and Fleetwood was no exception.

Paul's first job as Coxswain proved to be a baptism of fire and one which saw Paul and his crew in the spotlight of intense media coverage. "I was watching TV one night and it was blowing so hard that the windows were rattling and I remember thinking – this is not a good night for a turn out." Then the phone rang and Paul learned that the Ro-Ro vessel *Riverdance* from Heysham was in trouble off the Fylde Coast.

The official record describes the conditions as a Storm Force 10 gale with exceptionally heavy seas and a five metre swell. The wind gusted to 55 knots.

Paul followed his usual practice of moving the William Street astern out of the pen into the River Wyre from the outside conning position, which is open to the elements. "But as soon as I turned the boat to set off down the channel the weather hit us. I could not see a thing for rain and spray in that fierce wind."

The lifeboat battled out into Morecambe Bay where *Riverdance* had been hit by an exceptionally large wave about 10 miles off Rossall Point.

Approaching the Ro-Ro vessel *Riverdance*

This caused the cargo to shift, the engine to stop and gave the ship a 50 degree list.

"When we got there and lit up the scene with our searchlights I remember thinking how could that ship stay afloat with such a list? I expected her to turn over at any minute."

Paul had been able to select a particularly able crew that night from those who answered the call and arrived at the boathouse. One was David Eccles who talked on the radio to his fellow captain on the *Riverdance.*

The Fleetwood crew, who were joined by the Lytham St Annes lifeboat *Margaret Jean*, learned that the Master of the *Riverdance* had not dropped anchor because he considered it too great a risk to send his men out on the exposed foredeck to let the anchors go. As a result the ship was drifting helplessly at the mercy of the wind and waves. It was actually on a collision course with Blackpool's North Pier in a direct line.

An RAF helicopter from Valley in Anglesey winched 14 of the 23 passengers and crew off the Riverdance. The lifeboat lights helped them by providing a reference point in the pitch darkness.

Paul recalls: " It was not so much the waves and the swell that struck me, it was the force of the wind." As he manouvered the *William Street* up the side of a wave, one of the twin engines suddenly stopped as the propeller came out of the water and raced wildly but Mechanic Steve Carroll quickly got them going again.

Lifeboat *William Street* standing-by Ro-Ro Vessel *Riverdance*

Like so many victims of the Fylde Coast sands, *Riverdance* shifted ever nearer to the coast and finally ran aground at Cleveleys – just yards from the seafront.

Both lifeboat crews came back to Fleetwood but Paul and his team were back at sea within a few hours to stand by the stricken ferry while the rest of the people on-board were helicoptered off.

Riverdance, which was eventually cut up for scrap where she lay, became a tourist attraction and the lifeboat crews found TV cameramen and news reporters waiting to get their side of the story when they finally returned to Fleetwood for the second time. The incident was international news.

Riverdance ashore at Anchorsholme photograph John Dales

During his time as Coxswain, Paul recalls other services like navigating through the middle of the offshore windfarm in the middle of the night to take a disabled yacht in tow.

Another that sticks in his mind concerned two men taking an old motor cruiser from Holyhead, North Wales to Glasson Dock, in March 2011. Weather conditions had worsened and their old craft, not in the best of condition, had broken down. "We passed them a tow line and it was made fast in a bridle right round the wheelhouse which was the strongest part of the boat. The two men remained on-board and the tow back to Fleetwood began.

" You keep looking back to check that everything is OK and suddenly I saw the wheelhouse break free of the deck and go over the side. That disconnected the tow and pitched one of the men into the sea."

Quickly, Paul and his crew moved to successfully rescue him and lifeboat-man Dave "Skip" Frith went on-board the casualty and re-secured the tow rope which passed through a cleat in the bow and was then made fast around the engine as the strongest point available.

" But the tow acted like a cheese wire and it cut down into the structure of the boat near the bow. The man who had been overboard had also cut himself which needed further first aid so I spoke with the coastguard and we left that wreck on the bottom of the Irish Sea and came home." The boat was called *Beverley Rose* and the owners had bought it on e-Bay two days before. They were twenty five miles from land when the lifeboat found them and the motor cruiser had no navigational aids.

Paul, who is now 62, is still involved at Fleetwood Station where he can still command the boat in an emergency if colleagues are not available through work commitments.

And he's not the only lifeboat-man in the family. His son Chris, who also worked in the family plumbing and heating business, developed an interest and started coming down to the lifeboat station at the age of 20. He became a crew member and decided on a complete change of career as a deck officer in the merchant navy – training at the Fleetwood Nautical Campus of the Blackpool and The Fylde College which has strong links with Fleetwood RNLI.

Paul said: " I am proud of him and he's still involved when he's home from sea – a very useful member of the crew.

Tyne Class Lifeboat *William Street* (47-038) was on station at Fleetwood from 1989 until she was replaced in June 2016.

Lifeboat *William Street* photo John Dales

Fleetwood Lifeboat William Street *photo John Dales*

8 LIFEBOAT *'KENNETH JAMES PIERPOINT'* (2016 +)

The Shannon class all-weather lifeboat arrived on station at Fleetwood in June 2016 and at a service of dedication on 23rd June at Fleetwood Marina was named *Kenneth James Pierpoint.* The lifeboat was named in honour of a young RAF pilot who died during World War II.

Lifeboat *Kenneth James Pierpoint* photo Stephen Musgrave

As a strategic response by the R.N.L.I. to increasing its range of coverage to 100 miles from the coast the speed of the Shannon class has been increased to 25 knots. Formerly, a life-boat's hull had a usable life expectancy of twenty five years, beyond which a lifeboat would normally be retired into the reserve fleet or sold out of service. The construction of the Shannon lifeboat's hull is of carbon composite and the life expectancy is doubled to fifty years. With this new type of lifeboat on station at Fleetwood who knows what rescues will be performed over this extended lifetime of this vessel?

The Shannon Class of lifeboats were designed by the R.N.L.I. and introduced into their fleet in 2013. The identification number of Fleetwood's new lifeboat named *Kenneth James Pierpoint* is 13-14. Thirteen indicates the length in metres and 14 means the fourteenth lifeboat of this class. This lifeboat is 13.6 metres long, with 4.5 metres beam and of shallow draught, needing just 1 metre of water to remain afloat. It is self-righting with a displacement weight of 18 tonnes and carries 6 crew securely strapped into sprung seats to reduce the shock and impact of heavy seas. The operational speed is 25 knots and its range and endurance is 250 nautical miles. Powered by twin 13 litre Scania D13 650 horse power diesel engines there are no propellers and the engine thrust drives twin Hamilton HJ364 waterjets that provide propulsion and manoeuvrability.

The hull, deck and wheelhouse are constructed from a composite of materials, mainly glass-fibres woven into cloth before infusion in an epoxy resin glass layered sandwich construct, with carbon-fibre strengthening in areas of high load. Shannon lifeboat 13-014 is the first to be wholly fitted out at the R.N.L.I's All-weather Lifeboat Construction centre at their headquarters in Poole.

An elevated upper steering position aft of the main cabin gives all-round open aired viewing and a separate steering position is below in the air-conditioned main cabin. This lifeboat does not have a conventional steering wheel in the main cabin and the boat's direction is controlled by a 'joystick'. Another feature of this lifeboat is the innovative Systems and Information Management System (SIMS) that is an electronic integrated bridge system that allows the coxswain and crew to monitor, operate and control the navigation, communication, radar and engine/hull control system functions from the safety of their seats. The SIMS systems are similar computers to those fitted in military aircraft and the processor units are duplicated to withstand a malfunction or failure, giving improved resilience. The system was introduced in the current Tamar class all-weather lifeboats and has been further developed and improved for the Shannon. Crew members are already familiar with the operation of SIMS as the D-class Inshore Lifeboat has a scaled down version of SIMS, with similar screen layouts and functions. Training has been given to all crew to ensure they are competent in operation of the system.

RAF Pilot Kenneth James Pierpoint

Kenneth James Pierpoint was born in 1922 and studied at Altrincham Grammar School. He was a keen student, who represented the school at rugby and earned a place at Cambridge University. At the age of 18, in the midst of World War 2, he joined the Royal Air Force having decided to delay going to University in order to serve his country. By the age of 19 he had qualified as a pilot and at 20 years old he was posted to 605 Squadron Royal Auxiliary Air Force (RAuxAF), then based at RAF Ford, near Chichester in West Sussex.

Douglas Boston Mk. III

On 28th August, 1942, Kenneth was the pilot and sole occupant of a Douglas Boston Mk. III aircraft that took off on a night-time training flight. Less than 10 minutes into the flight, the aircraft dived into the ground and exploded near Bognor, West Sussex. Kenneth was killed immediately. The subsequent enquiry determined that shortly after take-off the aircraft had been illuminated by search lights that were participating in an exercise. Kenneth was possibly temporarily blinded or had to evade the lights by diving.

The Royal National Life-boat (R.N.L.B.) *Kenneth James Pierpoint* was mainly funded by a legacy left to the R.N.L.I. by Kenneth's sister, Miss Kathleen Mary Pierpoint and was named in Kenneth's honour at its launch on 23rd July, 2016 at Fleetwood Marina. Miss Pierpoint passed away on 31 May 2012, leaving the majority of her estate to the R.N.L.I. charity in memory of her brother, Kenneth James Pierpoint. Miss Pierpoint, from Altrincham, Cheshire, specified that the gift was to be used towards a lifeboat in memory of her brother and, thanks to this act of kindness, RNLI Fleetwood have been allocated a Shannon Class lifeboat that replaced the Tyne class lifeboat, named *William Street* that had been on station since 1989.

The absence of traditional propellers and use of water-jet propulsion, complemented by shallow draught mean the design is ideal to operate in the shallower waters of Morecambe Bay where vessels are often stranded on sandbanks. With a 50% increase in speed and weighing 8 tonnes less than the current Tyne lifeboat it will be possible to cut down the time needed to react to emergency situations where every second is vital to saving lives.

The generosity of Miss Pierpoint in funding this lifeboat is seen as a wonderful act of kindness and a fitting commemoration of her brother.

Shannon class lifeboat *Kenneth James Pierpoint* Artist Ken Frost

Gary Randles coxswain 2013 – present time (2017)

It was a proud moment for Coxswain Gary Randles when he piloted Fleetwood's latest lifeboat up the Wyre channel on her maiden voyage.

Lifeboat Coxswain Gary Randles

The craft, with its jet-fighter electronic technology, is as far from the days of sail and oar as anyone can imagine.

And yet the sea poses the same challenges and hazards as it always did although the modern boat is better equipped to cope with them.

The men and women who take the lifeboat to sea now are children of a modern age in which technology is part of everyday life. But they are still volunteers, just like those early lifesavers – willing to risk their lives, if need be, in a bid to save a stranger.

The *Kenneth James Pierpoint* arrived in Fleetwood for the first time that night in company with the boat she replaced – *William Street.* As they cruised close to the beach beside the promenade there was a crowd there to welcome the new lifeboat. They had turned out as a mark of respect and appreciation for the work done by R.N.L.I. volunteers and recalled the days years ago when, however stormy the night, people would come to the lifeboat house hoping to hear news of a rescue in progress.

Gary explained: " The new boat is so much better than *William Street* – better speed, better safety and comfort for the crew and an amazing computer system which is similar to that used in a jet fighter."

The lifeboat crew members now remain seated whilst on passage with seat harnesses on shock mitigating seats that take the impact of the weather and the cabin is air-conditioned. Each crew station has a computer screen and Gary has oversight of his shipmates at work – handling navigation, taking the helm, tending the engines and communicating with the Coastguard, the casualty and other ships.

Another new feature is the briefing that takes place before the crew leave the boathouse at which key problems likely to be met on the service and tactics likely to be needed can be discussed.

When Gary and his crew brought the *Kenneth James Pierpoint* to Fleetwood from R.N.L.I. headquarters in Poole they had already completed a training session down there and then took five days, over-nighting in different ports, to come home.

One member was Gary's 25-year-old son Daryl who became a lifeboatman at the age of 17.

Gary said: " We've got a very good team of men and women at Fleetwood and now we've got the new boat we are all set for a new chapter in the story of the station."

The son of a Fleetwood fisherman, Gary was a teenager when he got a summer job on the Fleetwood – Knott End ferry service then run by the Seed family.

"I used to go in the lifeboat station next door and got talking to people there."

After leaving school Gary became a trawlerman himself working for 20 years for the Buschini family whose operational base was in Scotland, rather than Fleetwood. When that came to an end he worked for the

Fleetwood Nautical Campus of the Blackpool and The Fylde College, which offers various training courses to merchant navy officer cadets and offshore workers. The college has strong links with Fleetwood RNLI. Students and staff are involved as volunteers.

Then Gary went back to sea and is now a motorman looking after machinery on a specialised ship in the oil and gas industry in the North Sea. He and his wife Kirsty live in Fleetwood and have three sons.

When Gary is away, a command team is available to take the lifeboat to sea. It includes another former fisherman, Tony Cowell, whose family links go back to the early days of Fleetwood's proud RNLI story.

Shannon lifeboat *Kenneth James Pierpoint* Artist Ken Frost

FLEETWOOD LIFEBOAT COXSWAINS

Coxswain John Fox and Capt Edward Wasey. 1859-1862.

Coxswain J. Leadbetter. 1862-1870.

James Turner coxswain 1870 – 1876.

George Doherty coxswain 1876 – 1878.

Coxswain Robert Wright. Appointed 1878. Retired in October 1895 after 36 years, the last 17 years as coxswain. Awarded 2nd Silver medal to mark outstanding service.

October 16th, 1903. David Leadbetter became ill and Second Coxswain John Robert Leadbetter took the boat.

Summer 1909 David Leadbetter died having served as coxswain for 14 years.

John Robert Leadbetter appointed coxswain (1909). Retired in 1923 having served 14 years as coxswain and been on crew for 41 years.

William Wright appointed 1923. Served 10 years to 1933. (Accident in boathouse – died 4th June, 1945).

Jeffrey Wright appointed 1933. Retired 1948.

James Leadbetter took over 1948. Retired 31st December, 1953.

Herbert Rawcliffe took over December 1953. Five weeks later on 7th February, 1954 died in accident at sea.

Albert Wright appointed February 1954. Retired 1960.

Richard Wright (Cush) appointed 1960. Retired 1964.

Ben Bee appointed 1964. Retired 1969 (died August 30th 1994. Scipio. Ashes scattered Sept 10th 1994, (lifeboat William Street).

Roy Mitchinson appointed 1969. Resigned 1976.

David Scott appointed 1976 Resigned 1980

Ian Fairclough appointed May 1980. Retired 11th March, 1998

Chris Hurst M.B.E. appointed March 1994. Retired December 2007.

Paul Ashworth appointed 20th December 2007.

Gary Randles appointed 2013+

POSTSCRIPT

In this the twenty-first century the act of volunteering for the lifeboat and the generous giving of money through public donations remain true to the values established over a century and a half ago.

The risks and perils of putting to sea in a lifeboat remain, yet they are mitigated through the excellent design of the boats and the high standard of equipment and training.

For the crew members, men and women, who daily respond to the summons to the lifeboat station each call is special, responding at a moments notice to the interruption of daily activity by the explosive maroons or electronic pager, leaving work and family behind at an instant. This jolt undoubtedly brings an adrenalin surge that heightens responses, yet there is more that – in the same way that an engine comes to life when started, so the emergent property of the lifeboat crews capability becomes more than the sum of its individual members as the team work function operates. The crew train as a team, each with their individual role, bringing a capability not only to navigate, communicate and undertake sea rescues. The conclusion is that with the lifeboats and highly skilled crews the noble act of lifesaving as sea is in safe hands with the Royal National Lifeboat Institution.

It will be noted that Inshore Lifeboats that have been such a significant part of the lifeboat service since the mid 1960's, being used to save many lives in circumstances where a traditional lifeboat may have been unable to operate. They are not considered in this book as a separate story is justified to consider their role over the past five decades.

ABOUT THE AUTHORS

Dr Stephen Musgrave was born in Burnley, raised in Fleetwood Lancashire and now lives in Stalmine.

Having trained for a career at sea as a Merchant Navy Radio Officer he came ashore and taught in a mono-technic Nautical establishment that merged to become part of a Further Education College. Before semi-retiring he worked in Higher Education with the Open University as Acting National Director for a professional development programme for staff in the Schools' sector in Information & Communication Technology.

He holds a Ph.D in Telematics – the science of Computing and Electronic Telecommunications, with a specialist interest in Portal systems.

For twenty three years he was involved in the lifeboat service in Fleetwood, serving as Deputy Coxswain for 12 years. He received the Royal National Lifeboat Institution service award for the most meritorious rescue in the UK in 1984, in a Lifeboat under 10 metres, when a windsurfer got into difficulties in gale force conditions in Morecambe Bay.

His first book Volunteers of the Lifeboat Service gives a perspective of his time as a crew member and officer in the lifeboat service, and an account of his ancestors link with the lifeboat service in the nineteenth century. The focus is on 'people' aspects of the R.N.L.I. and the changes from the 19th to the 21st century.

David Pearce has been a journalist in the north west for the past 56 years and has always lived in his home town of Fleetwood. He worked in dockland as a boy and, as a local newspaper reporter, wrote about the fishing industry and its community through its heyday and decline.

That took him from Whitehall to the deck of a trawler at Iceland and on-board many other ships in between from inshore fishing craft to lifeboats.

He has been proud to count some of Fleetwood's lifeboat-men among his friends over the years and he and his wife Susan demonstrated their admiration and respect for the work of the RNLI in a practical way by working as volunteer fundraisers for 25 years.

David has a long-standing interest in local history and his knowledge has generated money for charity through talks, articles and productions staged by Fleetwood Folk Club. He helped to found the Fleetwood Museum.

David played a major part in the establishment of the Fishing Community Memorial on Fleetwood seafront and the Lost Trawlermens' Memorial in Dock Street.

He is a trustee of the Jacinta Charitable Trust which owns and operates the heritage trawler Jacinta in Fleetwood Marina. When the ship was able to visit maritime events around the British Isles with a crew of 16, his duties were in the galley.

24620284R00116

Printed in Poland
by Amazon Fulfillment
Poland Sp. z o.o., Wrocław